LAURA

COURTESAN & LAY PREACHER:

being a consideration of her life & legend as
recorded by those who knew her, and those
who wished to know her

BY

Anthony S. Drennan

Anthony S. Drennan
Belfast
2008

This, the first edition of Laura Bell Courtesan & Lay Preacher, is limited to 299 copies.

No. _114_ *Anthay S. Drennan*

Copyright © Anthony S. Drennan 2008

First published in the United Kingdom in 2008 by Anthony S. Drennan, 6 Barnetts Chase, Belfast BT5 7BF, United Kingdom

Anthony S. Drennan has asserted his right under the Copyright, Designs and Patent Act 1988 to be identified as the author of this work.

a CIP catalogue record for this book is available from the British Library.
ISBN 978-0-9521048-2-7
Typeset by the author in Adobe Caslon Pro font using Adobe Creative Suite 2, printed on 115g Munken Print White 18 paper. Prepared for printing in the United Kingdom by April Sky Design, Colourpoint House, Jubilee Business Park, 21 Jubilee Road, Newtownards, Co. Down BT23 4YH. Printed by GPS Colour Graphics, Belfast.

CONTENTS

LIST OF PLATES

INTRODUCTION

I am only too aware of the limitations of this monograph and that the reader might expect a larger and more rounded biography of Laura Bell. For a subject as sensitive as this it is perhaps not surprising that surviving evidence is painfully thin. A sentence or two or as little as the surname of someone who dined with Laura tracked down in an obscure autobiography of some long-forgotten Victorian gentleman is often all there is to be found. I have therefore restricted myself to recording the evidence and by way of emphasis occasionally indicating an aspect which deserves further research.

Where possible I have included quotations from, and references to, original sources. I have also, where there is insufficient evidence, resisted the temptation to speculate and fill in the gaps with suppositions or fictional passages. After almost three decades of researching Laura Bell, and having reached the limit of diminishing returns, I leave it to others more knowledgeable than I am in Victorian culture to put her life in perspective. In particular it is clear that Laura's influence on the politicians she entertained at 15 Grosvenor Square and her relationship with W.E. Gladstone require careful consideration and scrutiny.

The following have generously given permission for the illustrations to be used in this volume: portrait of Mrs Thistlethwayte by Buckner with kind permission of the Lady Ironside to use it on the front cover of this volume; portrait of Laura Bell as a child with kind permission of George Farnham; miniature of Laura Bell by Girard and the photograph of the Billiard Room Hertford House with kind permission of the Trustees of the Wallace Collection; portrait of Mrs Thistlethwayte as a nun by A. Clayton with kind permission of the owner and the Courtauld Institute of Art; carte-de-visite of Laura Thistlethwayte and reproduction of the Gladstone letter with kind permission of Sir William Gladstone, Mr Charles Gladstone, Lambeth Palace Library and Oxford University Press. Grateful thanks are also due to the Linen Hall Library Belfast for permission to reproduce in facsimile the first two gathers from *A Short Visit to Ram's Island*. I am most indebted to Sir William Gladstone, Mr Charles Gladstone, the Lambeth Palace Library and OUP for permission to quote from *The Gladstone Diaries*, and to Nelson Bell who allowed me to examine his copy of *A Short Visit to Ram's Island*.

My grateful thanks for personal information on Laura Bell to J.F. Burns, M.R.D. Foot, Dr H.C.G. Matthew, Jean Gilliland, the Earl Bathurst, The Lord O'Neill of Shanes Castle, Lord Crathorne, The Lord Ironside, Robin Thistlethwayte, Peter Thistlethwayte and Stephen C. Bell. The librarians and staff of the Linen Hall Library Belfast, the British Library including the India Office and Newspaper Library Colingdale, the Wallace Collection archives and Lambeth Palace Library have all been enormously helpful and patient with my queries.

For help researching and providing feedback on my manuscript my sincere thanks go to Jack Gamble, Wesley McCann, Peter Grainger and Sandy Kane — and to Amber Benson for her encouragement when I thought I would never finish the final draft. Many thanks also to Joan Erskine whose editorial insights and suggestions for revision significantly improved the finished book. Any errors or flaws in the book's structure, argument and interpretation are entirely my own responsibility.

Every effort has been made to trace and contact copyright holders. The publisher will be pleased to correct any mistakes and omissions in future editions.

Endless hours of often unrewarding research were undertaken to build up the Laura Bell story piece by piece, fact by fact, until one day I discovered a most curious book printed in Belfast. Henry Bell's *A Short Visit to Ram's Island* has only survived because it is in the Linen Hall Library Belfast Printed Book Collection, but I am the first person in decades to look at this little volume which holds no apparent significance or interest until a connection is made to the story outlined below. To one bibliophile at least it has become the most remarkable volume in the entire library, but in order to understand *A Short Visit to Ram's Island* and its significance, the story of Laura Bell must first be told.

Anthony Drennan
Belfast, November 2007

TO THE READER

Where possible I have included extracts from named contemporary authors. Victorian readers would have understood that these carefully worded recollections of Laura Bell were meant to be read 'between the lines'. To have paraphrased them in this work would have been to loose their underlying meaning. Furthermore some of these statements quite clearly contradict each other, often depending on the author's moral viewpoint. Without conclusive evidence one way or another I leave it to the reader to decide which version, and which interpretation, is closest to the truth.

1

FROM GLENAVY TO DUBLIN CASTLE
1831-1848

*It is like a story from the Arabian Nights, with
much added to it. And yet we have only counted
the tale of fourteen years*
— William Gladstone

If Laura Bell's life were portrayed as a work of fiction, in a novel
or a film, it would be dismissed as unbelievable: a prostitute in
Belfast, courtesan in Dublin, then in London as the greatest *grande
horizontale* of her generation. Such a notorious life would, in itself,
show Laura Bell to be a remarkable woman, yet, astoundingly, at
the height of her notoriety she married into London society and
became a lay preacher, delivering sermons to poor tenant farmers in
Scotland and lowly shop assistants in London. Then she embarked
on a relationship with England's greatest Prime Minister, the
nature of which — platonic or much more intimate — remains
unclear. And yet the few pieces of surviving documented evidence
do indeed confirm that many of the significant events of Laura
Bell's tale actually did happen, and that the story is so extraordi-
nary that it deserves to be told.

By its very nature, this monograph contains only a small
amount of information which is both true *and provable*. This is
because in the late 1840s the subject, a Miss Laura Bell, became
the leading practitioner in that oldest of professions, prostitution.

1

As the most famous courtesan of her generation, and acknowledged as such by the use of the euphemism *grande horizontale* to describe her, Laura skilfully covered her tracks and obscured the truth throughout her lifetime and beyond. Portraits of her such as those painted by Richard Buckner provide some evidence as to her remarkable beauty, but at the same time depict an enigmatic smile which, like her story, provides more questions than answers. All we are left with are the myths and legends surrounding her life as documented by those who met her, and passed on by word of mouth by those who would have liked to meet her. As a short biography it thus reflects both the truth *and what Victorians believed to be the truth.*

Of Laura Bell's origins few facts can be ascertained. The handful of magazine articles written about her usually gloss over the period of her childhood with the singular remark that she came from Glenavy, a village in County Antrim some twelve miles west of Belfast. Laura's complex family situation is both confusing and contradictory, but as her formative years underpinned many of the strange decisions and curious incidents in her later life, it is with her enigmatic childhood that we must begin our tale.

GLENAVY

Laura Eliza Jane Seymour Bell was the daughter of Robert Henry Bell and Laura Jane Seymour. Her date of birth has been variously claimed as 1829 or 1832, and from her recorded age of 44 in the 1881 Census of England it would appear she was born in 1837! Based upon her stated age on her marriage certificate and death certificate, and her documented birthday, 18 October 1831 seems to be the date Laura would have us believe.[1]

Laura Bell's presumed birthplace of Glenavy is also open to question. Certainly in the first two decades of her life the family lived at Bellbrook House just outside the town,[2] and Mr John Larmour (owner of the Glenavy Mills) confirmed that he stood

2

as sponsor at her baptism.[3] Glenconway, a small hamlet of half a dozen houses near Glenavy, has also been suggested as her birth-place,[4] or at least the claim was made that the family lived there.[5] However, this may be a confusion with the fact that Glenconway House was a shooting lodge owned by the Marquess of Hertford (her father's employer). In the 1920s Sparke claimed Laura was born in Newry, County Down,[6] but no other information was pro-duced as evidence and until proved otherwise this must be treated as apocryphal. It is most likely that she was born in Dublin just before the Bell family moved to Glenavy. In 1870 the question of her date of birth seems to have arisen but in this confusing refer-ence it is implied that proof (presumably by means of a baptis-mal register) would depend upon knowing the parish or street in which her father's house in Dublin was located, information which Laura was unable to supply.[7] Furthermore, William Gladstone commented in his diary in 1871 that Laura 'told me the singular story of her birth'.[8] No more information was forthcoming, and we are left to make what we will of this curious and frustratingly unclear statement. Although, as we have already seen, Laura was somewhat inaccurate regarding her age (and by implication the date of her birth) in the 1881 Census of England, her birthplace was also stated as Dublin. There seems no obvious reason to lie about this location and it reinforces the Gladstone statement implying that her origins were, however briefly, in Ireland's capital city. Notwithstanding these alternative possibilities, Laura Bell is consistently described as being from Glenavy, and that is certainly where she spent her childhood.

Laura Bell's mother Laura Jane Seymour was the illegitimate daughter of Francis Charles Seymour-Conway, 3rd Marquess of Hertford (1777-1842). The Marquess (Plate 1), who owned vast estates in County Antrim, lived a flamboyantly disreputable life in London and Paris and was regarded as a notorious rake: so such a scenario is not unlikely.[9] He was known as the Caliph of Regent's

3

Plate 1. *Francis Charles Seymour–Conway,*
3rd Marquess of Hertford

Plate 2. *Lord Hertford's villa in Regent's Park*

Park and built a villa there (Plate 2) wherein he could be entertained by his *seraglio* of mistresses and prostitutes, and on more formal occasions invite up to 600 distinguished guests to dinner. Concerning this crucial relationship some authors have confused Laura Seymour and her daughter Laura Bell, and also the 3rd and 4th Marquesses of Hertford, but three pieces of evidence reveal the true story.

Firstly, *Burke's Landed Gentry* for 1855 includes a remarkable entry for Frederick Thistlethwayte (Laura Bell's husband) as follows:

> Augustus-Frederick [Thistlethwayte], *b*. July, 1830; *m*. 21 Jan 1852, Laura-Eliza-Jane-Seymour, dau. of the late Capt. R. H. Bell, by his 2nd wife, Laura-Jane-Seymour, illegitimate dau. of the late Marquess of Hertford.[10]

The above genealogical entry was printed in 1855, at which time the 'late Marquess' referred to the third of that name.

Secondly, many years later Lord Congleton investigated the story respecting the family relationship between Laura Bell and the 4th Marquess of Hertford and concluded:

> If her mother had been, as she alleged, a daughter of the [fourth] Marquess of Hertford ... *he would have been exactly twelve years old when his alleged daughter* [Laura Bell's mother] *was born.*[11]

Since the 4th Marquess was born in 1800, it follows that Laura Jane Seymour was born in 1812. Given these dates her father must have been the notorious third Marquess, who would have been in his mid-thirties when she was born.

Thirdly, a portrait of Laura Bell, at one time in the Wallace Collection, has the following carefully censored contemporary inscription on the back:

> Laura Eliza Jane Seymour Bell, daughter of the late Captain
> R.H. Bell, of Bellbrook, Co. Antrim, by his second wife,
> Laura Jane _____, natural daughter of the late
> Marquess of _____.[12]

The missing names of Seymour and Hertford respectively in
the above statement are self-evident. In Victorian England the
phrase 'natural daughter' had a very specific meaning relating
to being born outside marriage, a reference to a daughter being
acknowledged as such by her father. Since in order for it to reside
in the Wallace Collection the portrait would have been purchased
by the 4th Marquess of Hertford, or his natural son Sir Richard
Wallace, the inscription is thus a Hertford family acknowledge-
ment of the family relationship with Laura Bell (see Fig. 1). This
is not as surprising as it might seem since not only did the 3rd
Marquess have an illegitimate son (Richard Wallace) and daughter (Laura Jane Seymour), but his wife Maria Fagnani was herself
allegedly the illegitimate daughter of William Douglas the 4th
Duke of Queensberry, whose sybaritic notoriety earned him the
memorable sobriquet 'Old Q the Rake of Piccadilly'.[13]

The above three pieces of evidence are consistent with Laura
Jane Seymour being born in 1812, illegitimate daughter of the 3rd
Marquess of Hertford (who was then thirty-five years of age). She
subsequently gave birth to her own daughter Laura Bell in 1831
when she was approximately nineteen years of age. Regarding Laura Jane Seymour's mother (and thus Laura Bell's grandmother)
nothing is known, other than the observation that the date of her
affaire with the 3rd Marquess was sufficiently unambiguous that he
was willing to acknowledge the subsequent birth of his daughter.
However, the above statements are false in the specific claim that
Laura Jane Seymour was the second wife of Robert H. Bell.

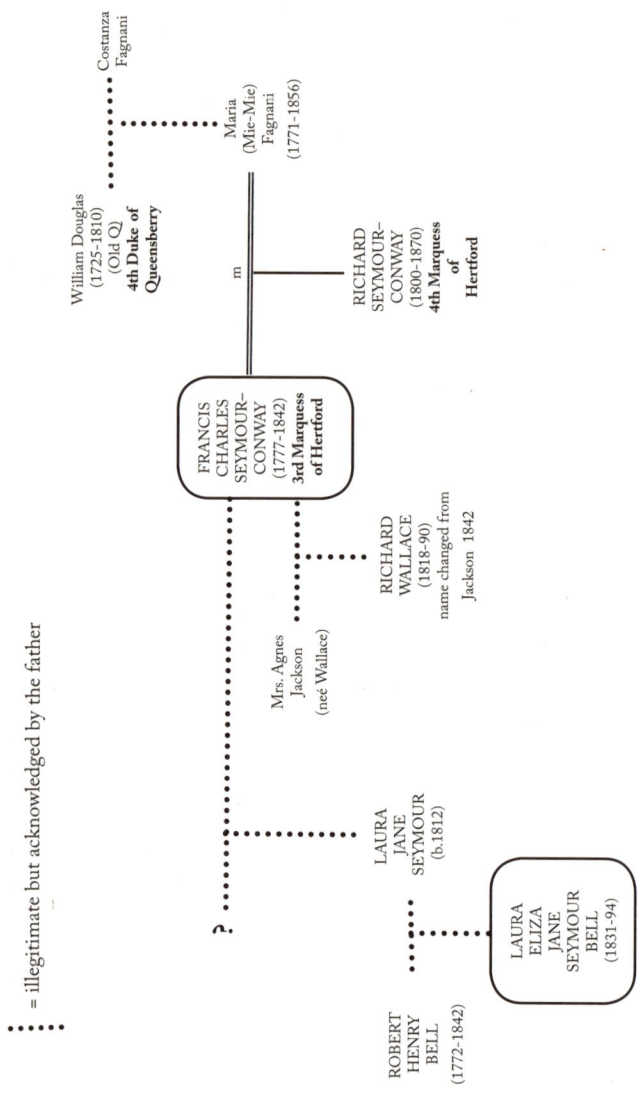

Fig. 1. *Laura Bell and the Marquesses of Hertford*

...... = illegitimate but acknowledged by the father

Costanza
Fagnani

Maria
(Mie-Mie)
Fagnani
(1771-1856)

William Douglas
(1725-1810)
(Old Q)
**4th Duke of
Queensberry**

m

RICHARD
SEYMOUR-
CONWAY
(1800-1870)
**4th Marquess
of
Hertford**

FRANCIS
CHARLES
SEYMOUR-
CONWAY
(1777-1842)
**3rd Marquess
of Hertford**

RICHARD
WALLACE
(1818-90)
name changed from
Jackson 1842

Mrs. Agnes
Jackson
(neé Wallace)

?

LAURA
JANE
SEYMOUR
(b.1812)

ROBERT
HENRY
BELL
(1772-1842)

LAURA
ELIZA
JANE
SEYMOUR
BELL
(1831-94)

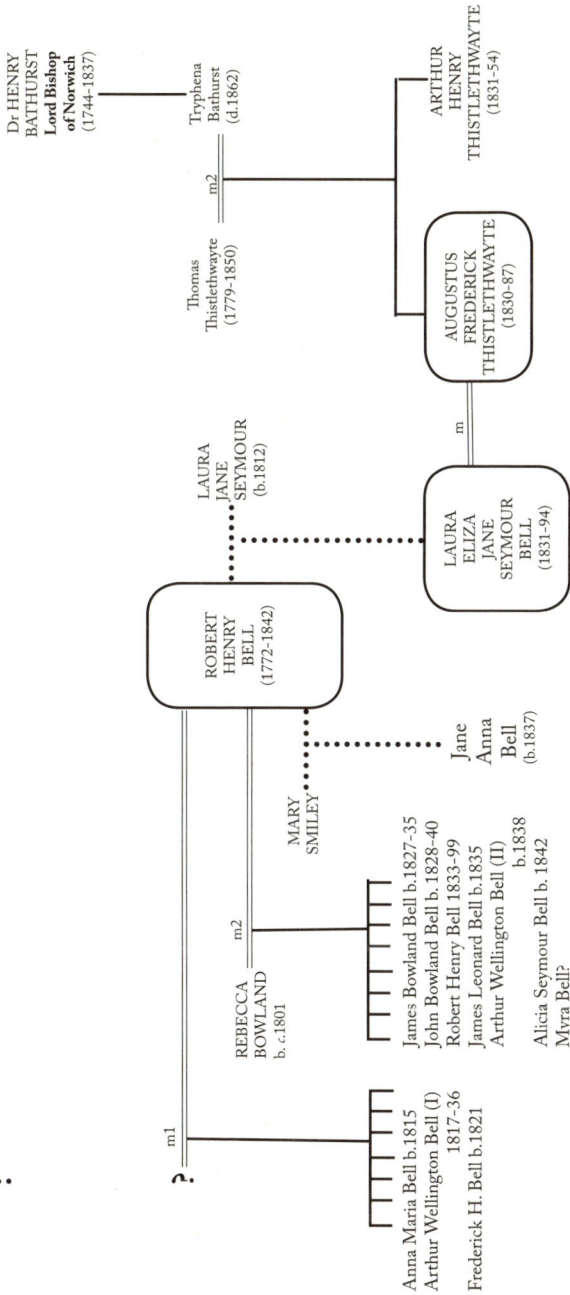

Fig. 2. *The Bell and Thistlethwayte families*

.... = illegitimate but acknowledged by the father

Dr HENRY BATHURST **Lord Bishop of Norwich** (1744-1837)

Tryphena Bathurst (d.1862)

Thomas Thistlethwayte (1779-1850)

m2

ARTHUR HENRY THISTLETHWAYTE (1831-54)

AUGUSTUS FREDERICK THISTLETHWAYTE (1830-87)

m

LAURA ELIZA JANE SEYMOUR BELL (1831-94)

LAURA JANE SEYMOUR (b.1812)

ROBERT HENRY BELL (1772-1842)

MARY SMILEY

Jane Anna Bell (b.1837)

REBECCA BOWLAND b. c.1801

m2

James Bowland Bell b.1827-35
John Bowland Bell b. 1828-40
Robert Henry Bell 1833-99
James Leonard Bell b.1835
Arthur Wellington Bell (II) b.1838

Alicia Seymour Bell b. 1842
Myra Bell?

m1

Anna Maria Bell b.1815
Arthur Wellington Bell (I) 1817-36
Frederick H. Bell b.1821

Robert Henry Bell (1772-1842) remains a shadowy and elusive figure in our story. Laura's later life required that her father appear as a respectable if minor figure in local society. It has been variously claimed that at one time he was an Irish constable,[14] or even a clergyman,[15] that he acted as recruiting sergeant for the East India Company,[16] was a Captain in the 4th Dragoon Guards,[17] had fought at Waterloo,[18] and most significantly as 'Lieutenant Bell' was a bailiff on the Irish estates of the Marquess of Hertford.[19] As the absentee landlord, proprietor and Lord of the Manor, the Marquess was not only the owner of Glenavy Parish but also of the surrounding parishes. In *Burke's Landed Gentry* (1855) Laura's father was posthumously identified as Capt. R.H. Bell of Bellbrook.[20] He appears in the list of subscribers to Lewis' *Topographical Dictionary* (1837) as 'Robert Bell, Esq., Bellbrook, Glenavy, Co. Antrim' — interestingly he did not include any rank, Captain or otherwise, against his name.[21] His obituary notice in the *Belfast Newsletter*, and those of three of his children, all include the title 'Captain' but no proof whether the rank was commissioned by the Army, Navy or other establishment is so far forthcoming. Perhaps the most confident statement on the subject comes from Isaac W. Ward, an authority on the social and political history of Belfast renowned for his skilled research and an obsessive accuracy in his writing. Under the pen name Belfastiensis his letter to the editor of the *Northern Whig* in 1903 includes the following confident statement:

> Laura Bell herself averred that this Captain Bell of the 4th Dragoon Guards was her father, but as a matter of history it was well known about Glenavy, where she was born, that her father was a Lieutenant Bell, who had been out in the service of the East India Company, and returned home to act for them in recruiting. He was employed at the same time in a dual capacity, as he was appointed a local steward

at Glenavy in connection with the Hertford estate office in Lisburn under the late Dean Stannus.[22]

Whatever the truth of his various titles (for which I have been unable to obtain any proof) and the various houses around and about Glenavy where the family reputedly lived, the key aspect of Robert Bell's life in relation to this biography was almost certainly his connection to the Hertford estates in County Antrim.

Information concerning Robert Bell and his domestic establishment is limited in scope and difficult to resolve. Family tradition claims that he married twice and that he had twenty-one children, but confirmational evidence is incomplete and there are gaps in the family tree which includes only eleven siblings (see Fig. 2). The family information is documented in Appendix A.

Nothing is known of Robert Bell's first wife — her name, where and when they married, where the family home was, how many children they had, all remain a mystery. The names of three of their children are recorded, of which Anna Maria was the only sibling with whom Laura is known to have kept in touch in later life — this may have been because Anna Maria and her family lived in London at the same time as Laura.

When a suitable romantic story was required, Laura was not averse to claiming that her mother had been a beautiful young maiden rescued in the nick of time from a Spanish convent by Captain Bell. To show her gratitude she rewarded Captain Bell by marrying him.[23] If this story has a basis in fact, it could well relate to a scenario where Laura's father married his first wife while serving in the army during the Peninsular War, but certainly not to Laura's mother. Whoever she was, Robert's first wife had passed away by 1822.

In August 1822 Robert married his second wife, Rebecca Bowland of Arklow, County Wicklow. The names of only six of her children, born between 1826 and 1842, can be identified

11

from the Glenavy Church records. It is therefore self-evident that (regardless of whether she was born in 1829 or 1831) Laura Bell was illegitimate, and Robert Bell was not married to Laura Jane Seymour at this time. The use of the four Christian names Laura Eliza Jane Seymour, three of which were her mother's full name, strongly suggests that her mother had a public relationship with Robert Bell. Furthermore, this liaison between the two lovers and the resultant birth out of wedlock was not a unique occurrence because in 1837 Robert Bell became the father of another illegitimate daughter, Jane Anna, whose mother was Mary Smiley. He acknowledged Jane Anna as his daughter in the Glenavy Church register.

Her illegitimate origins and subsequent childhood were to have a profound effect on Laura's psychological motivation and help explain several key decisions and actions implemented by her in later life during moments of crisis. The previously mentioned claim from *Burke's Landed Gentry* that Laura's mother Laura Jane Seymour was the second Mrs Bell must have been a lie. Laura's credentials were to accompany the entry for her new husband and his family in the primary genealogical reference book of English society, and it was therefore necessary to include a statement that established her lineage. By this time her father was long dead and the family scattered, most having returned to Dublin and some having moved to London or America. It was a bluff on a grand scale which stood a good chance of being believed. Once *Burke's Landed Gentry* innocently first published the lie of Laura's legitimacy they would keep republishing it in subsequent editions and no-one would question this bible of the English gentry.

During Robert Bell's first marriage the only geographical evidence is that their last son was apparently born at Bellbrook County Dublin. Building of the family home Bellbrook in the townland of Aghnadaragh outside Glenavy commenced *c.*1829 and the first family birth we know of to be registered in Glenavy

Parish Church occurred in 1833. This chronology is consistent with Laura Bell having been born as a result of an *affaire* in Dublin when Robert lived there with his second wife shortly before the family moved to their new house in Glenavy. The relocation was almost certainly instigated because of Robert's job as bailiff for the Marquess of Hertford. It explains the lack of family evidence in Glenavy prior to 1833, since this would instead have been recorded in Dublin church records which no longer survive. This conclusion seems to be supported by the claim that after her husband's death Rebecca Bell and those children still at home returned to live in Dublin in the 1840s.[24] The crucial relationship between Robert and Laura Jane Seymour at this time remains a mystery. All that we know is that Laura joined her father and his family at Glenavy shortly after her birth.

The most recent obituary in the *Belfast Newsletter* identifiable as belonging to the family is that of Robert Bell himself, who in his seventieth year died at Dundalk on his way to Dublin during August 1842, just three days after his last daughter, Alicia, was born.[25] From this information it appears that he was almost sixty years old, and Laura Jane Seymour in her late teens, when Laura Bell was born — a most striking difference in age. In conclusion all that can be said is that the evidence indicates a large and complex family history which is not yet resolved.

Laura went to a 'dame's school',[26] possibly the school at Aghnadaragh (the townland in which Bellbrook was built) which included a few female pupils, but more likely she was enrolled in Mary McGannity's School in Glenavy itself.[27] This was a pay school in a room in a private house, where in the mid-1830s there were seventeen pupils, all female. A neat cotton gown, straw bonnet, shawl, neat shoes and stockings and gloves were the usual dress for a young woman. The surviving sketch of Laura Bell as a child (Plate 3) certainly confirms this fashion observation, and underlines just how pretty she was. A survey of the Parish at this time noted that in general the children in the schools were particularly clean. Female children were sent to school until they could read and write, after which they usually went into service.

This somewhat cosy image of childhood may have been just that, since many years later Laura stated that as a child she lacked both training and regular discipline,[28] which makes her subsequent achievements all the more remarkable. In later life Laura was to claim in a very personal recollection that her whole childhood had been one of suffering,[29] and when she wrote her story for William Gladstone his reply to her included the following comments:

> Under the conditions of mind, and person, with which life was given to you, you were indeed sorely tried with storms commonly reserved for later life, and then for the most part arriving more rarely and with less violence.[30]

> All your childhood, deprived as it was of natural care and protection as well as of training and regular discipline, presents, in your pages, a picture of no other fault than that sort of wildness with which a plant of the forest is wild ... What you describe as a great and heavy sin of the child in the impulse of self–destruction did not, in my view, merit such a description. It was a natural recoil from unnatural evil in a creature too young to comprehend definitely the responsibility of this treasure and burden of life.[31]

> You blame yourself about going to the room: *undeservedly* if you were at the age I suppose. For a woman it would have been blameable.[32]

> It is like a story from the Arabian Nights, with much added to it. And yet we have only counted the tale of fourteen years. The poor dear child had suffered how sharp a winter

14

Plate 3. *Laura Bell as a child*

within indoors, before she was driven out upon the wide and wild expanse of life.[33]

The exact nature of the childhood incidents which provoked these comments is unclear, but Gladstone was sufficiently upset by the revelations to consider the effect upon the person who made a copy of Laura's autobiography for him, to the extent of asking Laura 'Have you not some fear of disturbing the mind of your copyist by your tale and its accompaniments'.[34] Certainly the spectre of child abuse, whether by someone in the family or a friend of the family, may be implied from the above quotations. Given what little we know of her early life it is an immeasurably unfortunate circumstance that Laura's manuscript autobiography disappeared from view when Gladstone returned his copy to the authoress.

BELFAST

Laura Bell left Glenavy when she was fourteen years old or perhaps slightly younger and travelled to Belfast where, according to the more imaginative yarn-spinners, she arrived in the gig of a neighbouring farmer with her worldly goods tied up in a striped counterpane. We do not know the precise reason why Laura left Glenavy but with a problem childhood, her father recently deceased (in 1842), and as half-sister to a very large family of brothers and sisters all trying to survive as best they could, Laura had few options available to her. It seems likely that a job in Belfast simply offered the best chance of survival in the harsh realities of Victorian society. Certainly she was both above the age of consent (which was twelve) and old enough to work for a living.

The Hertford family connection (with its potentially endless supply of Seymour relatives), in conjunction with her precocious beauty, intelligence and wit, were all that Laura had going for her but she certainly made the very best use of these attributes. Spending no more than two years in Belfast, perhaps a similar time in

16

Dublin, and a further year in London, Laura Bell progressed in these five years from the status of a country schoolgirl to that of the most famous courtesan in England.

Laura obtained employment in a Belfast store as a shop-girl, in the Mourning Department of a woollen draper's shop in High Street.[35] In the mid-1840s there were only two popular woollen-drapers in High Street — David McConnell at No. 68, and John Arnold at No. 45 who described his store as a Heimatemporium, no doubt in an attempt to impress his clientele.[36]

A key aspect of Victorian society and manners was the attitude to bereavement and mourning, and no one exemplified this more fully than Queen Victoria herself. The higher a person stood in society the more extensive the bereavement rituals, and hence the more expensive and elaborate the range of clothes required for mourning. Whether by accident or design, Laura soon found like others before her that the Mourning Department in a draper's store provided the perfect opportunity to meet suitable potential lovers. She was thus able to become acquainted with the upper-most strata of Belfast society with a minimum of difficulty, and as a result was able to supplement her meagre income by prostitution. Even at this early stage of her career, Laura showed the ability to be selective of her lovers, and was soon able to extract from them substantial sums of money and presents.

One of Laura's first conquests was reported to have been the owner of the draper's shop.[37] Their association came to a premature end when his wife discovered the liaison, but by then Laura Bell had realised where her true abilities lay and embarked on her legendary career as a celebrated *demi-mondaine*.

Laura had an *affaire* with a Captain of the Regiment of Foot, who soon tired of her.[38] She then attracted and captured the heart of John Moore, the eccentric owner of the famous stagecoach inn the Donegall Arms in High Street, who, it was rumoured, talked of marriage. Shortly afterwards a 'grave covenanting divine'

17

became her companion, and in later years she would claim that this unidentified young minister was the only real passion which lasted more than a month, and indeed that a change in lovers never troubled her for more than a week.[39] Her affair with a cousin of the Marquess of Donegall became another activity the gossips and busybodies could indulge themselves over, followed by tales of how she was able to string along an elderly ex-Sovereign of Belfast to whom, so the story went, she was almost engaged![40] The title Sovereign of Belfast had ceased in 1842, when it was replaced by Lord Mayor: so there were several ex-Sovereigns still alive in the mid 1840s, and it is unclear which was her lover.

Having won and rejected some of the leading military, political and religious gentlemen of the town, Laura now became embroiled in the first of her great crises. The cause and nature of this personal disaster are unknown but as a result she had to leave Belfast for Dublin. It has even been suggested that there was a suicide attempt at this time, or that one had at least been contemplated. This crisis was apparently the result of an incident involving a Major and his companion who saved her from an 'anonymous evildoer' who was struck with a sword. The Major and the Surgeon took Laura from near the Donegall Arms to her lodgings.[41] Whatever the incident was, it seems to have resulted in her isolation from the society in which she had gained a certain notoriety.

A solution presented itself for this lively bright-eyed young celebrity in the form of a career on the stage and everyone from censorious gossips to the gentlemen-about-town eagerly awaited the first steps of a great new actress billed as 'Laura Seymour' for two nights at the Old Belfast Theatre. But they were to be sorely disappointed. Laura was unable to remember her lines, and the stock company played an abominable practical joke to rid them of the interloper.[42] In an oblique reference to this incident on the stage, Gladstone commented that he was pleased 'that on the night of the appearance of Miss Dearlove there was no paint'.[43] Again the context is unclear, compounded by the coincidence that the artist who painted the scenery in the theatre at the time was a Mr Dearlove and perhaps implying that this was Laura's somewhat unsubtle stage name or the character she played.[44] Laura presented a sorry sight to her admiring audience, rushing off the stage at the first suitable opportunity:

> It was a failure that would have made other women shudder, but this gay butterfly turned it away with a snap of her fingers, a sparkle of brilliant eyes, and a light joke.[45]

And so, as suddenly as she had appeared in Belfast society, Laura Bell disappeared from both the stage and the town for ever, heading for Dublin, the promise of even greater monetary rewards, and the admiration she so eagerly craved.

DUBLIN

Within six months of her great crisis in Belfast, Laura Bell had become one of the most popular sights in Dublin, dazzling the public in her barouche pulled by fine prancing white horses. Henry Coke claimed that she appeared on the stage in Dublin, but in all probability this is a garbled version of her Belfast stage appearance.[46] She may even have appeared on stage in London many years later when Lady Elizabeth Pringle expressed misgivings, although whether the reappearance on the stage was considered or actually took place is unclear.[47] Laura, while she stayed in Dublin, was apparently known as Lady Hamilton the Younger[48] at this time and became the source of popular gossip with the inhabitants of the city. Her lovers included the famous Dr William Wilde, father of Oscar, who had a notorious inclination for very young women.[49]

Another of her conquests was an unnamed young officer from an important family who was on leave from his regiment, and who accompanied Laura to Queen Victoria's Great Review in Phoenix Park, in August 1849. Amidst the glamour of such a splendid occasion it says much for Laura's effect on people that Queen Victoria herself enquired of the Viceroy for Ireland as to the identity of this striking horsewoman taking part in the parade[50] — alas posterity does not record what reply he gave since it was whispered that Laura could sway the minds of the Viceregal Court, and furthermore:

> everywhere in the gay Irish metropolis one heard the name of a high dignitary coupled with that of the erstwhile Belfast shopgirl, and Dublin Castle, so it was hinted, held no secrets she did not know.[51]

Lord Lincoln (the future 5th Duke of Newcastle) was Chief Secretary in the Viceregal Court around this time, and may well have been the dignitary referred to. He and his family were to become lifelong friends with Laura and his acquaintance resulted in her friendship with the Prime Minister many years later. Furthermore, among the officers and aides-de-camp garrisoned in Dublin during her time there were those who became important friends when she later moved to London. The King's Light Infantry Regiment, which was headquartered there according to the *Army List for 1848*, included Lieutenant Conway Frederick Charles Seymour (a Hertford relative of Laura's) and Ensign Frederick Thistlethwayte, who within four years was to become her husband.[52]

This admission to the inner sanctum of British political power in Ireland must have greatly encouraged and focused Laura, making her aware of just how far she had progressed since embarking on her profession a remarkably short time before. It opened her mind to the possibilities of even greater earnings, fame and notoriety, and confirmed an affinity with politics and the corridors of power that was to laſt the reſt of her life. Having presumably achieved all she could in Dublin, with a tidy sum of money accumulated and a significant new colleċtion of ex-lovers and acquaintances from the higheſt level of society that Ireland could provide, Laura switched her attention to that ultimate goal, the conqueſt of London, in late 1849 or early 1850.

2

THE GRANDE HORIZONTALE
1849-1851

what strange stories I used to hear of her recklessness,
her prodigality, her luxury, and her cleverness
                                                    —Sir Francis Burnand

Using the technique so successfully mastered in Belfast, Laura soon found employment in Jay's General Mourning House, in Regent Street.[53] Such a position enabled her to meet the right people, and with her youth, beautiful form and piercingly memorable eyes, she soon attracted fresh admirers. In May 1850, while she was still working there, Laura Bell ensnared the man who would make her the most famous courtesan of her time — the Maharaja Sir Jung Bahadur, Prime Minister of Nepal and Commander-in-Chief of its army.[54]

Jung Bahadur lived in a Court where treason, poisoning, torture, intrigue and assassination were adopted by the King, Queen and courtiers as acceptable methods to achieve and maintain power. Jung was no exception — he murdered his uncle Mathbar Singh (who at the time was Prime Minister) when ordered so to do by the Queen. In the ensuing scramble for power Jung's chief rival Gagan Singh, who was the Queen's lover, was eliminated by a shot from an unknown assassin. The Queen took revenge by using Jung and his troops to wipe out several dozen opponents of the late Gagan Singh in an episode known to history as the Kot Massacre.

Subsequently Jung was appointed Prime Minister and Commander-in-Chief. He then had the Queen banished and the King abdicate in favour of the heir to the throne and from this point on he ensured that the real power in Nepal was concentrated in his hands, with subsequent Kings being rulers in name only.

Jung's visit to London in 1851 was the first by a ruler from the Indian sub-continent to be officially acknowledged as such by the British Government. They saw it as an opportunity to encourage Jung's support for the British at a time when there was increasing unrest in India which subsequently resulted in the Indian Mutiny. For his part Jung wanted the visit to emphasise and strengthen Nepal's independence from India and inspire him to implement changes to his country on his return home.

On his arrival in England Jung's modest entourage comprised some forty persons including two of his brothers, twelve guards, and four Brahmin cooks.[55] Having travelled overland from Khathmandu to Calcutta he departed the subcontinent in April 1850, and after stopping off for some sightseeing in Egypt (including a visit to the Sphinx) Jung Bahadur and his Nepalese entourage docked in Southampton on 25 May 1850.

The official programme for the visit included banquets held in his honour by the Duke of Wellington and Lady Palmerston, the Derby at Epsom, a gala performance at Covent Garden, and, at the invitation of Queen Victoria, attendance at the christening of the Duke of Connaught. He also enjoyed a visit to Scotland for some hunting and sightseeing. Jung and his brothers created a sensation whenever he attended a social event — his tunic was covered in emeralds, pearls, diamonds and rubies, he wore a golden sword and the dazzling display was topped off with a turban covered with rows of diamonds and emeralds and a feather from the bird of paradise. To avid English readers the journalists described him as the personification of the 'Mysterious East', someone out of the *Arabian Nights*.

One of Jung's engagements was meeting the Women's Association of England, and the ladies loſt no time in interrogating him on Nepal's culture and religions. When asked what he thought of British women he diplomatically replied that they enjoyed an environment of liberty and that they could live on good terms with their husbands, but rather aſtutely noted that gentlemen could not make a move without their wives' advice.[56]

Although officially residing at No. 1 Richmond Terrace, Jung Bahadur was besotted with Laura and provided a house for her in Wilton Crescent, next door to Canon Bennett of St Paul's Cathedral.[57] Alas, no evidence survives regarding the Canon's thoughts on his new neighbour. Laura, for her part, loſt no time in separating the Nepalese Prince from his wealth. In a period of only three months, not a single night as the gossips would have it, her skills as a *grande horizontale* earned her a quarter of a million pounds from her lover![58] At this time it was said that she once made an appearance at Buckingham Palace, and although Jung Bahadur spoke little English, there was even gossip of her becoming his Princess.

At the end of Auguſt 1850 Jung Bahadur travelled to Paris with Laura accompanying him on the usual tours of the Louvre, the Elysée Palace, Versailles and Napoleon's Tomb, and the couple were to be seen on fine Arab horses attending a military review at Satory near Paris.[59] However, while in Paris Laura apparently met an ex-lover she was ſtill attraćted to, or perhaps was abandoned by Jung who was seen in the company of Lola Montez and Fanny Cerrito, but whatever the cause the courtesan and the Nepalese Prince went their different ways.[60] Before parting company Jung Bahadur presented her with a magnificent ring, promising that if she ever needed help its return would bring him to her assiſtance.

On his return to Kathmandu Jung Bahadur was informed of an assassination plot which seems to have been hatched during his absence. The conspiracy was led by one of Jung's brothers and the brother of the King of Nepal. They planned to murder both the Prime Minister and King then take over control of the country as a pro-Indian and anti-British faction. In a strikingly similar plan to that adopted by the Indian Mutiny leaders they spread the rumour that while in London Jung Bahadur had committed the unpardonable sin of eating food cooked by non-Hindus. In fact it had been commented on back in London that Jung went out of his way to eat only fruit at these social engagements and later dine at home on meals cooked by his Brahmin cooks.[61] Furthermore, and closer to the mark, the conspirators claimed Jung had sexual relations with notorious European courtesans Laura Bell, Lola Montez and Fanny Cerrito.[62] Fortunately another of his brothers told Jung of the plot and the conspirators were arrested. He rejected calls for putting them to death, or for the 'lesser sentence' of blinding them with hot rods and cutting out their tongues, and instead had them jailed in India.

This gift of the ring and offer by Jung to come to Laura's assistance was taken up, and the tale was only to be concluded by the outbreak of the Indian Mutiny in 1857. What happened next depends on the version of the story — either Laura went to the India Office herself, or an official in that Department who knew the story of the ring contacted her.[63] According to the Duke of Portland, Laura gave the ring and Jung Bahadur's letter to a friend of his who took them to the India Office.[64] A near-contemporary newspaper even stated that the Secretary for India was the government official who called on Laura to request her assistance on behalf of her country. The newspaper reported that Laura declined the plea and it took a request from Queen Victoria herself to persuade her to return the ring to Jung Bahadur and ensure that his promise of assistance was upheld.[65]

Whatever the sequence of events, the India Office managed to return the ring to Jung Bahadur on behalf of Laura to remind him of his promise, and requested that the Nepalese Army side with

Great Britain in the Indian Mutiny, or at least remain neutral and not join forces with the mutineers. In the event both the Gurkahs and Nepal avoided a confrontation with Her Majesty's Government. Jung prudently decided that Nepal should side with the British and he even went as far as to accompany his troops as they fought. Furthermore, in an unbelievable postscript to the story, it was claimed that in order to appease and encourage Jung Bahadur the British Government refunded him the £250,000 that he had spent on Laura Bell in the hope that it would tip his decision in their favour.[66] Certainly he officially received a large area of land which the British Government restored to Nepal, and was awarded the Grand Cross of the Order of the Bath.[67] Thus, according to the gossips as they concluded this remarkable tale, the beautiful young courtesan Laura Bell played a key part in containing the spread of the Indian Mutiny and preventing India breaking away from the British Empire! A few years after the death of Jung Bahadur it was reported in a newspaper that Laura apparently requested the Star of India decoration as a reward for services rendered to crown and country, but not surprisingly the request was refused.[68]

Another variant of the story concerning the ring ascribes the Indian Prince role to Salar Jung of Hyderabad, and claims that Laura requested an audience with no less a person than the Prince of Wales, who acted on her behalf and spoke to the British Government. Furthermore Charles Dolph claimed in the 1920s that 'his late Majesty' (the erstwhile Prince of Wales) frequently told this story to his friends. Given Salar Jung did not visit London until 1876 (some nineteen years after the Indian Mutiny), and that the Prince of Wales was only fifteen years of age when he supposedly met Laura, this version of the story must be regarded as apocryphal.[69] In 1876 Edward Prince of Wales arrived in India and Jung Bahadur lost no time inviting him for some big game hunting in the Banbasa forest of Nepal (see Plate 4).[70] During the three-day tiger hunt Jung enthusiastically talked to Prince

26

Plate 4. *Jung Bahadur big game hunting with the Prince of Wales, 1876*

Edward about his visit to England some twenty-six years previously, and all the people he met. As the two mighty hunters sat
round the campfire in the evenings exchanging stories the Prince
learned about the legendary courtesan Laura Bell and Jung's ring
and promise. In turn this story was passed on by the Prince and
became the confused recollection Dolph spoke of some forty-five
years later.

In the early twentieth century a ladies' fashion journal mistakenly named Salar Jung of Hyderabad as Laura's far-eastern lover.
This was picked up by Wyndham, who realised it was the wrong
Prince and said so, but it was subsequently repeated and expanded
upon by Dolph. According to Henry Coke, Laura's Indian lover
was Dhuleep Singh, giving yet another variant of the tale. To com-
pound the confusion further this also was repeated by Dolph.[71]
Neither Salar Jung nor Dhuleep Singh stands up to scrutiny (they
would have been twenty-one and thirteen years of age respectively
and neither visited London at this time), and are clearly cases of
mistaken identity.

Jung Bahadur was keen for a second visit to England, but his
plans were thwarted at every step and it was not to be. Proposed
visits in 1862 and 1865 were cancelled because of the political
situation on the sub-continent and in particular Jung's unhappy
relationship with the British representatives in Kathmandu (Colonel George Ramsay and his successor). In 1874 Jung actually set
off and travelled as far as Bombay, but a fall from his horse resulted in a chest injury which postponed the visit once more. During
the 1876 tiger hunt the told the Prince of Wales he intended to
revisit England the following year. While out hunting in February
1877 Jung was taken ill with some unknown malady, slipped into a
coma, and died. He ruled Nepal for over thirty years and by siding
with the British when they needed him kept Nepal independent
from India. For the times his governance was relatively peaceful,
he gave the land its first written civil code of law and developed an

identity for the country which enabled it to deal with the British Empire. Yet he never forgot the exotic courtesan he lived with for a few months in 1850, and we are left to speculate how Jung and Laura might have conversed on his second visit to London.

Now Laura may have been abandoned in Paris by the Nepalese prince in 1850, but notwithstanding the competition from Lola Montez, Giulia Barucci and Marie Duplessis, she was soon living in Avenue Friedland, her new lover being no less a personage than the Emperor Napoleon III who spent thousands of pounds on her.[72]

Laura knew how to drop names and introduce intimate recollections into the conversation when an appropriate occasion arose. At the time of the birth of his son the Prince Imperial, Napoleon III was naturally concerned at his wife's state of health:

[Laura] used to tell a story of this time. When she asked the Emperor what he would have done if a daughter had arrived instead of a son, she says he replied, 'send it back!'[73]

Such gossip was not just appreciated for the wit displayed, but also for the repeating of an intimate moment of conversation with a suitably important figure in Victorian society. This liaison with the Emperor must have been of fairly short duration, however, and she returned to London where she was without rival as the leading *grande horizontale* of her age.

This phase of her life when Laura was at her most notorious is the time least documented by her contemporaries, and given Victorian attitudes it is not surprising that evidence is thin on the ground. As well as the aforementioned Jung Bahadur and Louis Napoleon, the Honourable Henry J. Coke claimed that Laura's reputed lovers included her uncle the 4th Marquess of Hertford, but provided no further details.[74] Other suggested lovers were the eminent Victorian gentlemen who attended dinner parties Laura gave after her marriage (see Chapter 4) but it is not surprising, given the nature of this small and exclusive group of powerful and self-protecting Victorian gentlemen, that there is no firm supporting evidence.

Reminiscences of Laura Bell from this period occasionally surface in the most unexpected places — such as the memoirs of eminent and somewhat staid Victorian gentlemen. In his 1904 memoirs Sir Francis Burnand wrote:

> As a 'boy about town' I remember several notorious Hetairæ being pointed out to me as they rode in spanking style in the Row, were driven in open landaus, or charioteered themselves about Hyde Park in the season. The most memorable of these was 'Laura Bell' … Clearly do I call to mind Laura Bell's pretty, doll-like face, her big eyes, not ignorant of an artistic touch that added a lustre to their natural brilliancy, and her quick vivacious glances as she sat in an open phaeton, vivaciously talking with a variety of men, all 'swells' of the period of course, at the corner of the drive near the Achilles statue, while her smart little 'tiger' stood at the horses' heads. What strange stories I used to hear of her recklessness, her prodigality, her luxury, and her cleverness![75]

As much as for any aspect or accomplishment, Laura Bell won widespread admiration for her riding ability which she displayed to maximum advantage in Rotten Row. Her impact when she entered a room was amply demonstrated at the Opera — she would delay her entrance until such time as she would be noticed. When she left before the end, swathed in her beloved jewels and on the arm of her current lover, the Opera would stop and the audience stand to watch her departure.[76]

According to Esmore, at this time she styled herself Laura Jane Seymour.[77] There was often the desire amongst the *grandes horizontales* to change their name in order to break family ties, either out of shame or in order to prevent any investigation of their background. Laura's adoption of her mother's name provides an example of the singular attitude which in retrospect so distinguishes her from her rivals in the world of the *demi-mondaine*. Only gentlemen of the highest position and wealth were permitted to visit Laura's establishment in Wilton Crescent (sometimes identified as Wilton Place), to be acknowledged as she rode past in Hyde Park, or to be invited to her box at the Opera. A curious event was recorded about this time:

> Before she married, Laura Bell had a house in Wilton Place, where she received her gentlemen friends, like a modern Aspasia or Phryne. The late Marquess of _____ was a noted figure there, and he often came on his white pony. The pony was carried off one day by a preconcerted arrangement, and was not recovered without a handsome reward.[78]

It is difficult not to read into the above statement that Laura was involved with, or colluded with, this pecuniary extortion.

T.H. Escott described Laura as the greatest beauty of the age and her portrait photographs were very popular with the inhabitants of the capital city; Horace Wyndham noted that such was Laura's popularity that a boot polish manufacturer reproduced one of her portraits to advertise his wares.[79] Such was her repute that the song *Laura, Laura, We Adore Her* was performed in music halls and pantomimes, and sold by street ballad-mongers.[80] Topical songs of her exploits could be heard sung by J.W. Sharpe, the star comedian, at Evans' Supper Rooms and Music Hall in Covent Garden.[81] It has been claimed that the virtuous heroine in the novel *Pendennis* was named after the less than virtuous Laura Bell by W.M. Thackery, but this must be regarded as coincidence. The novel was published in monthly parts between November 1848

31

and December 1850, and the evidence suggests that Laura only arrived in London in late 1849. Her first notoriety in the capital city would therefore have coincided with the end of the book's publication. Thackery had stayed in Belfast during his 1842 tour of Ireland but this was around the time Laura left Glenavy and before she commenced her notorious career. Yet Thackery portrayed the 3rd Marquess of Hertford (Laura's grandfather) as the wicked Lord Steyne in *Vanity Fair*, and it is not impossible that he may have heard of either Laura's exploits in Dublin or the Hertford family connection.

A comparison of Laura Bell with other courtesans of the nineteenth century draws out common themes, but also major differences which make her such a unique personality. Throughout the nineteenth century English courtesans such as Cora Pearl, Harriette Wilson, Catherine 'Skittles' Walters and Sophia Baddley, and their continental rivals Marie Duplessis, Apollonie Sabatier, Alice Ozy and La Païva inherited a unique niche in society.[82] Courtesans were the first celebrities and even if from humble origins had to be highly cultivated, to have an acceptable accent, and exhibit table manners and etiquette to fit in at the highest levels of society. An ability to interpret and predict their lover's moods and then to act accordingly, to be one minute a discreet companion and the next the outrageous courtesan, was the key to their success. Only someone with an innate cleverness and a natural skill to assimilate the required knowledge and culture could achieve the unassailable position of *grande horizontale* of their day.

One of the most obvious aspects of a courtesan was her chosen name. A change of name was a two-edged sword which could obscure the truth and disconnect the courtesan from the family. It could be used to save your family from shame, but as often as not was used to disown them and refute their very existence. Emma Elizabeth Crouch transfigured into Cora Pearl, the Irish-born Eliza Craigie into the exotic Lola Montez, Catherine Walters was clearly identified by the epithet Skittles, and Laura Bell herself when in Dublin was known as the euphemistic Lady Hamilton the Younger. Once she progressed to London, confidence and experience resulted in Laura using her mother's name Laura Jane Seymour which simultaneously disowned the Bell family yet signalled her link with the Seymour-Conways and the Hertford family to prospective clients.

The commencement of Laura's career in a woollen shop in Belfast was not unusual. Marie Duplessis started work in a garments factory, Céleste Vérard worked in a milliner's shop, and by the time she was thirteen Alice Ozy had been promoted from sewing in the back room of a fabric shop to serving behind the counter and had been seduced by the shop owner. Jay's General Mourning House where Laura worked when she first arrived in London was a few years later to employ the notorious Mabel Gray. Not only did a clothing emporium provide the ideal opportunity to meet suitable potential lovers, but it also provided the required knowledge of the clothing industry and fashion trends. In Paris the great French *grandes horizontales* were expected to set the fashion style — Cora Pearl's dresses were made by the same couturier as those of the Empress Eugenie.

The ability to act the part that was so essential to courtesans was often reflected in a love of the stage, although Lola Montez had no more success than Laura with an attempted career as an actress. Lola Montez was born Elizabeth Rosanna Gilbert in 1821 at Grange, County Sligo, Ireland. After several affairs with army officers she undertook a transformation into the sensational Spanish dancer Lola Montez and in 1843 made her debut on the London stage. Inevitably her appearance at Her Majesty's Theatre, although a triumph, prompted some of the audience to recognise her as the erstwhile Mrs Eliza Craigie (her married name) and she was forced to flee the country in disgrace. Travelling to Germany she unsuccessfully tried to hook Franz Liszt but struck gold when she began a liaison with King Ludwig I of Bavaria. The *affaire* lasted from 1846 to 1848 when she was at the zenith of her fame and notoriety. After the inevitable falling out with the King and fleeing from a hostile crowd enraged by her meddling in local politics, Lola Montez returned to London in 1849 just in time to see Laura Bell burst on the scene as the new queen of the *demi-monde*. In the autumn of 1851 Lola encountered Laura Bell at Rond Point on the Champs Elysées in Paris. According to contemporary newspaper reports Lola insulted Laura's waiting women and the result was a brawl between the two elegantly attired courtesans. Lola was badly punished by Laura, who on her return to London wasted no time in proudly informing everyone of her great victory.[83] Shortly afterwards Lola Montez left Europe for New York, spending most of her remaining years touring the United States, Canada and Australia, but the two women were to meet at least once again. In 1861, some ten years after the Paris incident, a *New York Herald* newspaper correspondent visited Lola Montez at her house in London, where he also encountered Laura Bell. According to this press hound the two women were the best of friends, indeed Laura had provided financial assistance to Lola, enabling her to lease a house in Park Lane and use it as a lodging house. He reported both women had become religious and were under the pastoral care of 'Great Tribulation' Cumming. This cosy image was somewhat tarnished by the further revelation that on the afternoon the reporter visited them both women copiously indulged in hot gin![84]

It is easy to ascribe a young girl's initial foray into a career of prostitution to an insufficiency of wages yet many of the courtesans exhibited the tendency to spend well beyond their means throughout their lifetimes, regardless of the vast size of their income, and it is no surprise that Laura was taken to court several times for being unable to pay large bills to milliners.

Publishing one's memoirs became a way for courtesans to avoid impending penury and destitution when in reduced circumstances in later life, but it could also be used as an act of revenge. Harriette Wilson's celebrated four-volume memoirs were a huge success when published in 1825, but they only saw the light of day after a number of eminent gentlemen were informed of the publishing venture and given the option to pay £200 to guarantee their excision from the work. The Duke of Wellington's refusal to play along with the money-making scheme resulted in the oft-quoted reply 'publish and be damned!'. Cora Pearl followed Harriette Wilson's example and former lovers were given advance notice of her 1888 memoirs. Céleste Mogador showed a poor sense of timing by publishing her memoirs just before her marriage. Her publisher insisted the publication went ahead and, although a financial success, it almost prevented the marriage. Laura Bell did write her memoirs, but unlike her rivals' they were only for the eyes of one person (William Gladstone). Given Gladstone's comments on the memoirs it is difficult not to suspect that Laura's manuscript memoirs were too honest and truthful for the time and they were deliberately destroyed.

Once past the height of their fame courtesans quickly faded from view due to a decreasing circle of friends and the lack of an established position in society. Some were more fortunate than others – when Païva and Marie Duplessis died they left not inconsiderable fortunes, and Apollonie Sabatier spent her last years in comfort thanks to a 50,000 francs per month allowance from former lover Richard Wallace when he inherited the Hertford family fortune. Uniquely among *grandes horizontales* Laura abandoned her career at the height of her fame to take on and succeed at the most difficult challenge it was possible to attempt — acceptance by the religious and political establishments as a reformed woman. This transformation was triggered by marriage.

THISTLETHWAYTES, MARRIAGE AND
A VISIT TO RAM'S ISLAND
1852-55

*The Island Queen — an honorary title, graciously
beſtowed on Mrs A.F. Thiſtlethwayte*

—Henry Bell

Laura Bell entered a new phase of her life when she became
attraćted to the Thiſtlethwayte brothers. The suitor who was to
become her husband was Auguſtus Frederick Thiſtlethwayte,
whom she moſt probably firſt encountered in Dublin, after he
joined the King's Light Infantry in 1846 and before he retired from
the Army in 1850. His younger brother Arthur Henry Thiſtlethwayte commenced his Army career in 1849. Their parents were
Thomas Thiſtlethwayte Esq. MP, of Southwick Park, Hampshire,
and his second wife, Tryphena Bathurſt.

On 16 January 1827 Tryphena Bathurſt married Thomas
Thiſtlethwayte, the ceremony being performed by her father Dr
Henry Bathurſt, Lord Bishop of Norwich. Henry wrote to his
daughter the following day, describing his new son-in-law as 'our
moſt excellent friend'.[85] It might be presumed that, as Bishop of
Norwich, Henry would have a position of considerable influence
and ſtanding within the English eſtablishment but he showed his
individuality by writing a pamphlet on toleration towards Roman
Catholics in Ireland for which he was heavily criticised and
which, it was suggeſted, impeded his further promotion within

the Church of England hierarchy.[86] It was only as an old man that he was offered, and refused, the Archbishopric of Dublin.

On the Bathurst side of the family the other character of note was Tryphena's brother Benjamin who was carving out a promising career as a diplomat when, as an Envoy Extraordinaire to the Court of Vienna, he mysteriously disappeared in 1809.[87] Notwithstanding investigation by both the British Government and the Thistlethwayte family, evidence of Benjamin Bathurst's demise was not forthcoming. Various unsubstantiated theories were proposed — it was believed he was travelling incognito to avoid capture by the French or the Russians, or may simply have been the fatal victim of a highway robbery.

The Thistlethwayte family wealth was based upon land at Portsmouth, which had been expensively purchased by the Government in order to build a fort for coastal defence. Their other property was only some 500 acres, but since this was in London between the Bayswater Road and Edgeware Road, it provided a not insignificant income. The family was thus well to do with important relatives and a position in Victorian society.

The Thistlethwaytes and Bathursts provided the social standing that Laura Bell required and needed if she was to retire as a *grande horizontale* but remain in the heart of London society. There is no evidence as to how Laura's marriage was received by the two families, although the inclusion of two Thistlethwayte beneficiaries in her will many years later suggests that at least some of her new relatives accepted her recently respectable, or at least acceptable, status.[88]

By 1851 Laura had become the lover of the younger son Arthur, who by this time was serving in the Scots Fusilier Guards. Since his relative Lord Bathurst lived in Wilton Crescent (the street where Laura had lived with Jung Bahadur) this may well be where they first met. Esmore claimed that this relationship was 'solely of a commercial nature',[89] although subsequent events suggest a more meaningful friendship. Thomas Thistlethwayte died in 1850, leaving only £300 a year to Frederick and the bulk of his wealth to his younger son Arthur.[90] This division of the father's fortune would seem to have accounted for Laura's initial interest in Arthur, but on 21 January 1852 Laura Bell married Frederick Thistlethwayte at St George's, Hanover Square, London.

The motives behind Frederick's proposal and Laura's acceptance we shall probably never know — it was generally believed that he was besotted with her and married on impulse. Given Laura's fame, fortune and highly profitable lifestyle it seems likely that another great crisis forced Laura's hand — certainly from the outset the marriage was fraught with difficulty. Laura later revealed that from the start the marriage had been a disaster, a 'compact extorted by violence'.[91] Jean Gilliland has suggested an unwanted but subsequently aborted pregnancy as the cause of matrimony.[92] Perhaps it was just that Laura was sufficiently astute to realise that her career had peaked and decided that marriage to a suitable candidate, and with it a form of respectability, would permit the possibility of a long-term continued association with the people she admired. As might be expected, the Thistlethwayte honeymoon was spent travelling in Europe, visiting Switzerland, Germany, Italy and France. They were observed at Homberg in Germany by Henry Vizetelly:

> There were two players at roulette who every morning were punctually in their places when the kursaal flunkey arrived with the treble-locked oak-bound chest containing the notes and specie which the officials hoped would suffice for the requirements of the day. These were the wealthy Mr. Thistlethwaite [sic] and the notorious Laura Bell, whom he had recently married … The pair sat day after day at the table courting fortune with a patience which Penelope might have envied.[93]

PORTRAITS

Once married the young Mrs Thistlethwayte soon set about having her portrait painted, and the various surviving examples produced over subsequent years show a remarkable variation in both style and interpretation.

The most memorable portrait of Laura Bell is the undated oval miniature on ivory by Ernest Girard. Wearing a lace-edged shift, and with pearls in her hair, she enigmatically studies a note from her lover (see Plate 5). This beautiful portrait is to be found in the Wallace Collection, having been obtained by Laura's uncle the 4th Marquess of Hertford, or his son Richard Wallace. An indication as to the esteem in which Laura was held by at least some of the Seymour-Conways is a surviving photograph of the Oval Drawing Room at Hertford House c.1897. It shows a wall display of fifty-one miniature portraits, the central one being the Girard miniature of Laura in a striking ornate gilt frame.[94]

The painter who made the most of Mrs Thistlethwayte was Richard Buckner, who painted her some seventeen times between 1853 and 1870 at a cost of over £1,000.[95] Although they were all painted after her marriage, and the subject therefore named as Mrs A.F. Thistlethwayte, it did not stop the suggestion that Buckner was one of Laura's lovers.[96] The reason for her popularity as a sitter was explained by Mrs Godfrey Pearse, who in 1926 wrote:

Buckner is a portrait painter whose work is considered of little account nowadays. He was a *habitué* at Lady Essex's and when we first knew him had made a great success by his portrait of a celebrated *demi-mondaine*, Laura Bell, a beautiful woman who closed a varied and public amorous career by marrying Mr. Thistlethwayte, a Hampshire squire. Although the period was mid-Victorian, which is nowadays dismissed as a time when every-body put their heads in the sand like ostriches, the *beau monde* flocked to Buckner's studio to see

39

the portrait — and it brought him many commissions from ladies of the moſt impeccable reputation.[97]

A photograph of the Billiard Room at Hertford House (ascribed a date of c.1897, but possibly as early as c.1888) shows a large portrait of Laura in full-length riding habit and hat with a pet dog at her side (Plate 6). According to Richard Buckner's account books this was his moſt expensive portrait of Laura, coſting some £157-10-00 in Oĉtober 1854.[98] The painting was sold by Chriſtie's Auĉtion House on 27 June 1913 (item 52) and its laſt known owner was the American colleĉtor Francis C. Harper c.1935-7. Its present whereabouts are unknown but a black and white photograph of the portrait survives in the Witt Library of the Courtauld Inſtitute (Plate 7). Although painted when Laura was twenty-three years of age, juſt over a year after her marriage to Frederick Thiſtlethwayte, one can ſtill see in the portrait evidence of the doll-like face and large eyes which made such a ſtriking effeĉt when she went riding in Rotten Row as the moſt famous courtesan of her day. Yet after examining the piĉture for a moment the viewer becomes aware that the exaĉt centre of the composition is her wedding ring and is left contemplating how well, or whether at all, Laura ſtuck to her marriage vows.

Another Buckner portrait of Laura has remained in the Thiſtlethwayte family. The large eyes are once again evident, but are balanced by 'the beautiful shoulders for which in her springtide, she had been famous'.[99] At one time this ſtriking portrait was re-produced as a print and a small photograph of it was found in an old envelope in room 9 Hertford House during July 1945.

At the Royal Academy in 1871 Buckner exhibited item 1149, yet another portrait of Laura Thiſtlethwayte (see the front cover of this volume). Now some forty years of age, Laura's eyes are ſtill pre-eminent but as expeĉted from an evangeliſt the shoulders are now covered by a gauzy shawl. The portrait was painted at the zenith of

Plate 5. *Laura Bell by Ernest Girard*

Plate 6. *The Billiard Room at Hertford House — the portrait of Laura in hunting dress can be seen on the wall*

Plate 7. *Laura Thistlethwayte in hunting dress by Buckner*

her relationship with Gladstone, and indicates how compelling a figure she would have been to him at this time. According to Lord Ironside the portrait was exhibited in Glasgow by his father-in-law in the early 1930s.[100]

To the remaining portraits and sketches there are few references. A half-length portrait of Laura in a shawl was at one time said to have originally been in the Wallace Collection,[101] then owned by Murray Scott *c.*1897, Lady Victoria Sackville *c.*1919,[102] and subsequently purchased and reproduced in the *Sphere* magazine in 1927.

Perhaps the most curious portrait was that painted by Alfred Clayton, which depicted a head and shoulders portrait of Laura Bell dressed as a nun (Plate 8). According to Horace Wyndham it was reproduced extensively and preserved in Victorian scrapbooks by young women who presumably knew nothing of the model's history (although this claim may refer to another portrait of Laura with the title *Madonna* which was painted by Buckner). To a viewer unaware of the identity of the sitter in the portrait, Clayton's painting would lose much of its meaning and all of its notoriety — an effect seen again in the apparently uninteresting booklet *A Short Visit to Ram's Island*.

The new name Mrs Augustus Frederick Thistlethwayte did not induce a change to conformity and a settled lifestyle in Laura — within six months of her marriage she ran away with her brother-in-law Arthur.[103] Around this time the Ram's Island Incident took place, but as events turned out there was to be no long-term relationship between the lovers.

THE RAM'S ISLAND INCIDENT

The episode of most relevance to bibliophiles is known as 'The Ram's Island Incident', which occurred in the summer of 1853. Ram's Island is less than a mile long and very narrow, lying in Lough Neagh about a mile from the shore and a further two miles

Plate 8. *Laura Bell as 'The Nun' by Alfred Clayton*

from Glenavy. The island was first mentioned in the year 1056 in the *Annals of Ulster*, its one feature having been a church (which no longer exists) with a round tower which in Victorian times had survived to a height of some forty-three feet. When Lord O'Neill of Shane's Castle bought the island from James Whittle of Glenconway he built a hunting lodge beside the tower (Plate 9). His Lordship created numerous walks on the island, and the Cottage (as it was known) was both elegant and filled with costly furniture.[104] By the 1850s, therefore, Ram's Island was an idyllic setting with romantic ruins and a place where friends of Lord O'Neill were invited to stay. As far as Laura was concerned the island provided the ideal location, being very close to the old family home and friends, but equally importantly providing the privacy she and her London companions could luxuriate in.

Although by the summer of 1853 Laura was married to Frederick Thistlethwayte, this period is in the middle of the hiatus between Laura running off with her brother-in-law Arthur in the summer of 1852 and his death in the Crimea in the autumn of 1854. Between June 1853 and August 1854 (when the Royal Scots Fusiliers sailed for the Black Sea and the Crimea) Arthur's regiment was stationed in Dublin.[105] It would have been a simple journey for Arthur to ride up from Dublin to Ram's Island to visit Laura for a few days in July or August 1853. Certainly at this time her notoriety was at its zenith and her lifestyle at its most reckless. It therefore seems probable that she returned home to Glenavy with her lover and not her husband — certainly the description of the party of friends who accompanied Laura does not suggest that her somewhat dull and religious husband was present as he would not have approved of such people. The story is only recorded by Alfred Esmore, and is transcribed here in full:

> Most people would rather forget the life of Laura Bell during the year or so that succeeded these strange nuptials.

Plate 9. *Lord O'Neill's Cottage, Ram's Island, Lough Neagh*

She developed just about this time a fancy to revisit the haunts of her childhood. In the bosom of Lough Neagh lies Ram's Island, green, and containing within its circumscribed confines the ruins of one of the ancient round towers which have occasioned so much discussion as to their original use. Formerly the habitation of a fisherman, Ben M'Areavy, this island was sold for £10 to the lord of the adjoining shore, Lord O'Neill of Shane's Castle, whose pastime consisted of yachting in Lough Neagh. Under his ownership a neat lodge was erected on Ram's Island and game of various kinds introduced. It was a resort that any Nature lover or sportsman would glory in.

Now, strangely enough, a member of the neighbouring family — the Pakenhams of Langford Lodge — had also married a Thistlethwayte, and by a curious coincidence also, her initials were identical with those of our heroine, Mrs Laura Thistlethwayte. With this understood, then, what more natural could happen than that Lord O'Neill, one morning receiving a scented note from a 'Mrs Laura Thistlethwayte', should be deceived as to the real identity of the sender. His fair correspondent graciously craved permission to enjoy a brief holiday occupancy of Ram's Island. His lordship, with the characteristic hospitality of his much-respected family, warmly welcomed the intending visitor, and moreover, placed his yacht at her disposal.

Ten days later, Laura Bell set her dainty *bottined* feet in Glenavy again, but this time as the aristocratic Mrs Thistlethwayte, of Grosvenor Square, and with an entourage that would have been in keeping with the style of a Chicago millionaire on his travels. They were lively days indeed for Ram's Island and the normally quiet district.

The party consisted of as choice an assemblage of the brightest spirits as might be collected in a week's tour of

London — patrons of the turf, supporters of the prize-ring, devotees of the gambling-table, languid lovely beauties of burlesque, who claimed renown from their disregard of conventional life.

She appeared in pastoral *tableaux vivants,* danced the tarantella to perfection, woke up the echoes of Glenavy's groves as her tandem bowled along, organised rustic sports, and paid visits to old acquaintances — including the late Mr James Charters, of Glendona. She delighted everyone, and the farmers of the neighbourhood forgot even their markets to assemble and see what high times those 'wonderful gentry from London' were enjoying. For the nonce the reality of Ram's Island challenged the romance of the paradise of *Rasselas.*

Fast enough, however, Lord O'Neill was discovering the identity of his pseudo-aristocratic guest, and when she had shown signs to outstay her welcome, along came a peremptory message which left the lively coterie with no other resource than to flit back to London, leaving Ram's Island to resume once more its natural quietude.[106]

It certainly would not have escaped the notice of the local inhabitants that the penniless child who left Glenavy some ten years previously for a life of prostitution and degradation was now returned at the invitation of Lord O'Neill. The excuse that Laura had been confused with another Mrs Thistlethwayte of local origin seems unlikely but the claim that there were two women with the same name approximated to the truth. Laura's father-in-law Thomas Thistlethwayte had, by his first marriage, eight daughters and two sons — the eldest of whom was also named Thomas. This Thomas, half-brother to Laura's husband Frederick, in 1850 married Elizabeth Catherine Packenham of Langford Lodge, County Antrim. Thus a point could be stretched and a confusion occur between the two Mrs Thistlethwaytes, both sisters-in-law and from the same area of County Antrim. The owner of Ram's Island, John Bruce Richard O'Neill (1780-1855), had been created Baron O'Neill of Shane's Castle in 1793 and 3rd Viscount O'Neill in 1795. Although Lord O'Neill was seventy-two years of age at the time the 'Ram's Island Incident' occurred, he had held the post of Constable of Dublin Castle since 1811 and it seems unbelievable that he was unaware of either Captain Bell and his family history (Glenavy is only nine miles from Shane's Castle) or Laura's escapades in Dublin where one of her lovers had been an important dignitary in Dublin Castle itself. Even so, to accept this most fortunate defence by Lord O'Neill that he confused the two women argues a remarkable degree of ignorance on his part as to which woman he was in communication with. Given the notoriety the visit raised, it does seem very much to be an attempt at an excuse, and justification of an error of judgement, after the event.

This brief tale would have remained just that, another in a long list of incidents in a particularly eventful life, if it were not for a small and apparently uninteresting book I discovered in the Linen Hall Library which remarkably confirms the story. The book has the title *A Short Visit to Ram's Island, Lough Neagh, and its Vicinity in the Year MDCCCLIII*, ostensibly written by a Henry Bell, and printed for him by A. Welsh of 10 Arthur Square, Belfast, in 1853 (see Appendix B which analyses and reproduces the first eight leaves of the book).

The work comprises a mere thirty-two pages in total, and most of these are notes to fill out the volume. The purpose of the book is actually to record a song lyric by Laura Bell called *The Island Queen* and the popular air *Bonny Portmore* with which to accompany the lyrics. The remainder of the book is a series of little appendices by Henry Bell — notes on the locations and references contained in the lyrics to *The Island Queen*, subjects of historic interest in the neighbourhood, a poem *The Wren* by Henry Bell (in the Scottish dialect), and a postscript by him praising the Rev. James Stannus and 'the judicious and liberal concurrence of our esteemed landlord the Marquess of Hertford'! These items add to the couple of important pages in the slim volume, but with the exception of the extracts reproduced below provide little of interest to the story.

The most notable aspect of *A Short Visit to Ram's Island* is that surviving copies have been systematically censored (see Appendix B). Words (and partial words) have been carefully scraped off the page and replaced with a ruled line. The censored items would be impossible to reconstruct without making the connection to Laura Bell.

The frontispiece comprises an oval frame of leaves and flowers, hanging from which is a bell with the initial 'H', presumably signifying that Henry Bell was the artist. There is, alas, nothing inside the oval and no indication that anything was originally affixed to the page. The expected item would be a portrait of Laura as *The Island Queen*, but proof awaits the discovery of further copies of the book.

The leaf after the title page leaf contains on one side a dedication, and on the other side the lithograph 'Ram's Island'. The dedication reads as follows (the excised words being indicated by _____):

The following pages, descriptive of scenery and localities in the North of Ireland, and interesting reminiscences connected therewith, have been written and compiled at the particular desire of an esteemed friend, _____, for _____. This little book _____ by _____ Henry Bell.
The Grove Cottage, Near Lambeg, Lisburn, Ireland.
15th September, 1853.

It is uncertain what the missing words are, and, again, the answer will only be determined when an uncensored copy of the book is found. Whether Henry Bell was a relative of Laura is unclear, but this seems likely. Clearly he had been invited to join the Ram's Island party and produced this booklet as a memento of the summer's entertainment.[107]

The page after the dedication contains a frontispiece lithograph of Ram's Island. The sketch (reproduced in Appendix B) depicts the island with its striking Round Tower, and between the trees the roof of the Cottage can be seen. There is the suggestion of a boat on the Lough, presumably Lord O'Neill's yacht. In the foreground are two lovers, their arms entwined. It is difficult not to speculate as to the identity of the couple — the woman obviously represents Laura but the other ought to have been her husband, probably was her brother-in-law, and possibly could have been any of her other lovers! One suspects that there is a story behind this drawing, but its significance was hidden from anyone not in Laura's intimate circle of friends.

The poem/lyrics *The Island Queen* is prefaced by the following explanation:

The Island Queen
Mrs. A.F. T_____'s Farewell to Ram's Island, Lough Neagh, on the occasion of her departure for her residence in London, after having spent some weeks in Lord O'Neill's Cottage, on the Island, in the autumn of MDCCCLIII.

Only someone aware of the Laura Bell story would recognise that A.F. were the initials of Laura's husband Augustus Frederick and that the censored word was Thistlethwayte, which is again excised in one of the notes that follow the lyrics:

The Island Queen

An honorary title, graciously bestowed on Mrs. A.F.
T_____, by the residents of the neighbourhood, on
the occasion of her welcome visit to this interesting locality
— the home of her fathers.

We unfortunately have no opinion on the above sentiments
from the residents in the neighbourhood. What can be said is that
it created a sensation — the notoriety of this infamous woman
tricking Lord O'Neill, (the senior Peer in the district), and the
reckless and dissolute lifestyle that she evidenced during her stay,
kept local gossipmongers in business for months. The lyrics to *The
Island Queen* begin 'Farewell Ballinderry, and dear Aghalee, Ram's
Island – its Round Tower, and old Ivy Tree' the lines being reminiscent of the popular song *Ballinderry*. In a late Victorian book
on Glenavy the author, writing about Ram's Island, commented
on the popularity of *Ballinderry*:

When Mr and Mrs Hall visited Glenavy, during the
preparation of their work on 'Ireland', they often heard in
the neighbourhood a song descriptive of the beauty of the
Island, the refrain of which ran –

'It's pretty to be in Ballinderry,
It's pretty to be in Aghalee,
But prettiest of all in bonny Ram's Island,
Sitting under the trysting tree.
Och hone! Och hone!'

The song was a year or two ago revived and much sung in
London drawing-rooms.[108]

The book ends with a lithograph of the music *Bonny Portmore*
in a leaf border and is followed by Notes relating to the lyrics and

a Postscript neither of which adds anything to this story. From my analysis in Appendix B it seems likely that the specific identification of Mrs Augustus Thistlethwayte in this little booklet had to be censored to prevent its use as evidence of an adulterous affair with her brother-in-law in a possible divorce case.

ARTHUR'S DEATH

Laura and her brother-in-law could not have spent more than a year or eighteen months together as lovers because Arthur, as a young officer in the Scots Fusilier Guards, was shipped off to Turkey in the summer of 1854 in time for the first great battle of the Crimean War. Having sailed to the Black Sea in *The Golden Fleece*, the Scots Guards marched towards Sebastopol in atrocious weather, with many falling sick from cholera, heat and want of water. The regiment encountered the Russian Army in the first engagement in the Crimea, the Battle of the Alma. Of this action the *Belfast Newsletter* was to report on 18 October 1854 that:

> Amongst the many daring exploits of the intrepid men by whose energy and unshaken courage the allied arms have been carried to the heights of The Alma, we have not heard of an instance which surpasses in cool daring the conduct of Lieutenants Lindsey and Thistlethwaite [sic] of The Scots Fusilier Guards, the Queen's colour being carried by the former and the regimental colour by the latter gentleman.[109]

The events were captured even more dramatically in the words of Alfred Esmore:

> Next day was to see a deed of valour which still lives as golden page in history. Then, September 20th 1854, two young officers of the Scots Guards — one carrying the

Queen's colours, the other the regimental colours — were specially conspicuous by their bravery in that mad infuriated rush known as the Battle of Alma. For his share of the pluck young Lindsay, afterwards Lord Wantage, received the Victoria Cross. What of his equally daring companion? When morning dawned it was found that he — young Thistlethwayte, the brother-in-law and close companion of Laura Bell — had died the hero he had proved himself the day previously. When his corpse was found stretched out on the bloody escarpment it was seen that locked in his death's embrace were his dearest treasures — the colours of his Sovereign and a miniature of the wretched woman he loved.[110]

The *Belfast Newsletter* 18 October 1854 claims Lieutenant Thistlethwayte was unhurt in this incident. A memorial to Arthur Thistlethwayte in the family church at St James-Without-the-Priory-Gate, Southwick, states he died at Scutari Hospital on 26 November 1854, a month later. Given their relationship it would not be impossible for Arthur to have carried a miniature of Laura. The conflation of the battle and deathbed scenes would have provided a better telling of the tale — and where Laura was concerned it is not uncommon to find the tale taking precedence over factual precision.

A consequence of this glorious death was that the fortune Arthur received as an inheritance on the death of his father now passed to his brother Frederick. Laura had thus lost her current lover, and in what might be seen as her most cynical act she wasted no time in returning to live with her husband.

Before they met Laura, the Thistlethwayte brothers had been living in Curzon Street,[111] and after Laura's marriage to Frederick the couple moved to Westbourne Terrace.[112] Runaway lovers and glorious deaths not withstanding, within two years Frederick and Laura moved to 15 Grosvenor Square, where they spent the remainder of their married life. This move may well have been an attempt by husband and wife to get their troubled and eventful relationship back on the rails again. It certainly engendered a most surprising transfiguration in Laura Thistlethwayte.

4

EVANGELISM AND ENTERTAINING
1856-1863

a well-known preacher in her day was
the notorious Laura Bell

—Sir John Robinson

In 1856 Laura Thistlethwayte shocked and astounded her many ex-lovers (and would-be lovers) when she renounced her erstwhile profession, announced a religious conversion, and embarked on a new career preaching and saving souls! According to a newspaper correspondent Laura's husband spent two or three years preaching after being converted by Richard Weaver, a semi-professional pugilist who became a much-loved evangelistic preacher.[113] It is therefore not surprising his new wife would consider a new career, but would execute it in her own independent and inimitable style. Brownlow North, brother of Lord Guilford, was one of the most famous evangelists in the wave of revivalism that took hold in the early 1860s and his example was said to be a key inspiration to Laura, perhaps because of his profligate and indulgent lifestyle before his conversion.[114] Brownlow North (1810-75), after leading a dissolute life, had a dramatic spiritual experience in November 1854. From his home at Elgin (some thirty-five miles from Inverness) he began distributing religious tracts to the working classes, his first sermon being to shoemakers in 1855. The catchment area for his endeavours would have included the Thistlethwayte country residence near Loch Luichart. Laura's religious conversion and first sermons at Dingwall (some ten miles from Inverness) would seem to have been inspired by her hearing Brownlow North preach in the Highlands.

Laura decided to use her husband's country residence near Loch Luichart in Ross-shire as the location for her initial preaching ventures. The house was rented from Lady Ashburton, whose niece Mary St Helier recorded society's view of these events in her *Memories of Fifty Years*:

> About the same time that Mr Brownlow North was rousing the country by his revival meetings, a very powerful rival appeared on the scene in the person of Mrs Thistlethwaite (the celebrated Laura Bell), who, having married a Mr Thistlethwaite, a man of large fortune, had come with her husband to Loch Luichart, a deer forest belonging to my uncle, Lord Ashburton, which they had taken for a term of years. At first the county looked askance at the new arrivals, and she was not visited. Rumours which reached my grandmother's ears of her extreme repentance and great spiritual gifts, backed up by an entreaty from my aunt, Lady Ashburton, that she would recognise her tenant, produced a great sensation in our family; and, after many consultations and heartburnings, my grandmother consented, in order to please my aunt, to receive Mrs Thistlethwaite. We children were all sent out of the house the day when she paid her first visit, and only gathered from the mysterious whisperings of the maidservants that someone who ought not to have come to the house had been there, and that we had been sent out of the way to avoid meeting her.[115]

All her married life Laura induced this dichotomous reaction when appearing in society, as either someone to whom one should not be introduced because of her notorious past, or who should be supported in spite of it as a result of her religious transformation. Sir John Robinson neatly summarised the quandary with the phrase 'a well-known preacher in her day was the notorious Laura Bell'.[116] Laura began conducting revival services in the local Free Church buildings, and Lady St Helier continued:

> The services were not very well attended at first ... But after a time curiosity got the better of discretion, and people flocked from all parts of the country to hear her discourse. The internal surroundings of the church did not lend themselves to any emotional effect, but Mrs Thistlethwaite, beautifully dressed, and standing at the end of the building, so that all the light which entered through the small windows was thrown on her, illuminating the spot where she stood, poured out an impassioned address, not eloquent nor convincing, but certainly effective. She spoke with great facility and with a good deal of emotion in her voice, and an evident air of sincerity and personal conviction. This, added to the remains of very great beauty, an influence largely increased by her great generosity to the poor people, made a vast impression on her congregation, and after the first meetings she succeeded in producing all the effects of other revival preachers, and many conversions were supposed to have been the result of her ministrations.[117]

and concluded:

> She was a very striking-looking woman, and the large black mantilla which covered her masses of golden hair, the magnificent jewels she wore round her neck, and the flashing rings on the hands with which she gesticulated, added to the soft tones of a very beautiful voice, made a great impression on those who listened to her.

She was joined afterwards by Lord and Lady Kintore, Lord Kintore being a very religious man, and he and Mrs Thiſtlethwaite conducted services for many weeks; but the conversions of which they boaſted were not many, nor, I fear, very permanent.[118]

Encouraged by this rural success, Laura tried to hold a meeting in the county town of Dingwall, but the crowd turned up from a sense of curiosity, the local miniſter and elders criticised her, and it was not a success. This incident resulted in correspondence reprinted in the *Inverness Courier*, including the following letter from Laura and dated 4 October (year unknown):

Dear Sir,
You will favour the cause of truth by kindly ſtating in your next report that I have not appeared in any pulpit here. At the requeſt of many I have, through grace, humbly declared the plan of salvation by faith in a risen Saviour, the Lord Jesus Chriſt, — my objeĉt being to enlighten the poor and not the rich. Dr. Begg and Mr. Kennedy are both ignorant as to what the true Church of Chriſt is founded upon. It certainly is not bricks and mortar, but living ſtones, bought with the precious blood of a Lamb without blemish ...
    A sinner saved by grace through faith in
    the Lamb of God, L Thiſtlethwayte[119]

A Ross-shire journal reported in 1862 as follows:

Mrs. Thiſtlethwayte preached at the Free Church of Garve on Sunday week to an immense assemblage. The congregation was composed of people of all classes, but chiefly of the more intelligent; it was eſtimated that there were about forty carriages in attendance.[120]

The segregation of the congregation by means of the euphemism 'the intelligent class', together with the quantifiable carriage
count, succinctly enabled the journalist to identify for the reader
the significance of the upper-class people present at the sermon,
and needed no further elaboration. A remarkably gossipy article
headed 'Lady Evangelists' appeared in the *Wesleyan Times*. The
editor introduced the article thus:

> A correspondent sends us the following particulars with
> reference to the accomplished Mrs. Thistlethwayte, whose
> ministrations have been the means of accomplishing so
> much good not only amongst the upper classes of society
> and her own sex, but amongst all sorts and conditions of
> men. We have ourselves known men, bigoted Papists, awe
> struck by the fervour of her appeals, whilst the case and
> elegance of her style, as well as many peculiar circumstances
> connected with her, have all tended to give her a leading, if
> not the first, position among lady evangelists.[121]

The article, apparently by a minister whose pen name was
Young Humphrey, gives a remarkable flavour of the times and
people's attitude to the evangelistic Laura, and is therefore quoted
at length:

> I know the lady very well, and I know something of her
> eventful and interesting career, in great part from her own
> lips. I believe she is the daughter of an Irish clergyman. In
> person she is of moderate stature, well made, good figure,
> and fair complexion. Her manners are very modest, timid,
> and winsome. The expression of her countenance is most
> affectionate and pleasing. Her eye is very fine, mild in its light,
> and pure, full-formed, and full of questionings: when she

61

looks at you the feeling is at once excited that there is some
sweet thought or emotion flowing limpidly and tranquilly
through her mind. Her disposition, I should say, is frank,
open, and playful; perhaps originally gay and sportive, even
to a fault. But it is chastened now; controlled and disciplined
by Providence and grace. She is immensely kind, confiding,
and generous; and would, I believe, do anything, or suffer
anything, rather than not be useful and do good to people.
She sows her seeds beside all waters, but she often feels
obliged to halt between the monitions of prudence and the
impulsions of zeal. Her heart decides, for her instincts and
passive faculties are stronger than in those whom education
and the world has made calculating. The predominance
of feeling exhibits itself in her public utterance. She is
intensely earnest and conciliating, and, except when she is
expounding, she never becomes argumentative or critical;
but she beams upon her audience with an intense love which
win the submission of 'the pure in heart', and dismays the
superficial scorner into silence and self-contempt. Her dress
and gesture are chaste, plain, and unostentatious; the one
symbolical of the other, and both of her mind. Occasionally
she is lost for a fit word; and sometimes you feel that she is
bringing matter to the text; but you don't feel uneasy, — you
are assured it will come out in the end all right. I think she
is about from thirty to thirty-five years of age. I have met
with few Christians to surpass her in the even and efficient
impulse to do good in spite of a supercilious and gainsaying
world. I believe she is well supported by her gallant husband,
who belongs to an old Hampshire family whose seat is near
Portsdown Hill, Fareham. He is an officer in the army; was
in the Crimean campaign, and has been out of commission
from ill health ever since he came home. He is very wealthy,
has preached a few times, but is of very retired habits. When

I went to travel in the Winchester and Wickham Circuit, I found this lady and her husband living at Wickham Hall, having hired it for a year while their own house in London was being refitted. To my astonishment I found that they did not attend the Parliamentary institution, but our little obscure conventicle. This was a great scandal to all the Church magnates — My Lady This, and General That, and Colonel The Other, who lived in the village and neighbourhood, and of course our poor little flock of peasants were mighty set up, and with good reason, for we were never in want of funds for chapel purposes as long as they continued with us. But they were generous all round, and gave all sorts of things to all sorts of people, good, bad, and indifferent, visiting them, and breaking the bread of life everywhere. I was invited to the Hall frequently, and always found myself in the midst of wealth there, but I also always felt myself in the presence of devout people, whether they were alone or others with them — indoors and outdoors they were the same …

In our first conversation, I found that Mrs. Thistlethwayte had frequently addressed young females in the Institute at Marlborough Rooms, and I proposed she should preach in our village chapel. She shrank from this, as she had never preached at all — only given addresses, she said, and never to a mixed congregation. However, I prevailed upon her to do so. We had a splendid service. People came from far and wide, and even the most obstinate bigots from the Church contrived to squeeze themselves within the door. She continued to preach for us again and again, with increasing power and fruit, before she ever ventured forth beyond our village. So that the United Methodist Free Church at Wickham must have the credit of bringing this accomplished 'lady evangelist' through her novitiate. Since that time — about three years ago — she has gone forth like a burning and shining light, first to the navvies at Portsdown fortifications, then among the canny Scots, then again in Paris among the neglected English stable-boys, and where else I don't know. Both herself and her husband have 'Plymouth brother' proclivities; but they are slight. She is more of a Methodist than anything else. She prefers our hymn-book to any other, and she sticks to her Methodist lady's-maid, and doesn't know what she would do without her.[122]

As well as the United Methodist Church in Wickham, Mrs Thistlethwayte could also be heard at the Literary & Scientific Institute in Edward Street Portman Square, at Exeter Hall and at the Polytechnic in London.[123] Then, with the owner's permission, she began to hand out religious tracts to shop assistants in large West End stores, inviting them to prayer meetings at her home in Grosvenor Square. Charles Dolph remembered seeing Laura in Paris in the 1870s, living in the Upper Avenue Friedland and doing a lot of preaching.[124] Addressing the general public at Speakers' Corner in Hyde Park was apparently less successful. While out walking near Marble Arch 'a well known peer' came upon Laura while she was being heckled and obviously frightened, and escorted her back to Grosvenor Square.[125] It is a telling incident in as much that no one was with Laura at the time, neither her husband nor friends, and exemplifies her self-will and determination. Another example caused almost as much difficulty:

At a midnight meeting on one occasion an incident happened that rather disconcerted her. She was speaking of the folly of a life of sin, when a girl called out 'Come, come, Laura: *you* haven't done so badly.'[126]

These incidents were exacerbated due to Laura's inexperience

in speak   c, and not being practised in dealing with
unsymp;   ing. She clearly preferred having carefully
controll   with selected (or at least restricted) audiences.
The and   or of *Fifty Years of London Society* reported:

She   he most remarkable women of the latter
par'   enth century. Her intellectual capacity was
alm   nal and to this was added a very poetical
im;   e artistic element in her nature and her
generous impulsiveness culminated in her development into
an ardent missionary. One of my friends, feeling some doubt
as to her power as a lay preacher, went to hear her address
a crowded audience at the old Polytechnic. Great was his
astonishment when, instead of giving a rhapsodical recitation
of the familiar description, Mrs. Thistlethwayte delivered
an address consecutive in its argument, and, granting her
premises, brilliantly illustrative... Her appearance on the
platform of the Polytechnic was a realisation of beauty and
art. She had fair hair, luminous, glittering eyes, and a superb
figure. Her dress on these occasions was of black silk, and
her sympathetic, pleading voice never failed to stir even
those who were most unwilling to yield to the influence of
a woman speaker.[127]

Sir Willoughby Maycock recollected:

I well remember taking my late lamented mother to hear her
preach at the Polytechnic in the summer of 1874, where she
drew packed houses. She was getting on in years then, and
inclining to the obese. But the lustre of her beautiful eyes,
her most distinguishing feature, was only surpassed by the
sparkling of an array of large diamond rings, which adorned
her fingers, as she raised her hands in eloquent exhortation

to her audience to follow the path that alone leads to salvation; and she impressed us both with the sincerity of her conviction.[128]

and Sir Willoughby continued with another of those singular reminiscences of Laura that populate such biographies:

> Only recently the custodian of the Paddington Cemetery, where her body lies, told me he once had the privilege, in the later 'eighties, of extracting a fly from one of those beautiful eyes, in recognition of which service Laura presented him with the sum of seven shillings and sixpence, which left a lasting impression on his mind.[129]

The generous reward may be explained by the presumption that the unnamed funeral was in fact that of her husband Frederick Thistlethwayte at Paddington Cemetery in 1887.

With her astounding determination and will to achieve her goals that we have come to expect, Laura managed to ingratiate herself with a key group of Plymouth Brethren called the Welbeck Street Section, but this success almost became her downfall. The Welbeck Street Mission in Marylebone included members of powerful families such as Roden and Darnley. Some of their relatives had known Laura in her notorious days, and so two members of this religious circle, Lord Congleton and Admiral Fishbourne, were despatched to Ulster to discover the truth concerning the origins of Laura Bell.[130] John Vesey Parnell, Lord Congleton (1805-83), was a cousin of Charles Stewart Parnell the leader of the Irish nationalist movement. In 1830, shortly after joining the Plymouth Brethren, he founded a meeting room for them in Dublin and spent most of his life travelling and preaching. Lord Congleton was minister of the Welbeck Street Chapel from 1860 to 1883 and history regards him as a simple-minded enthusiast with gentle manners and a retiring disposition.[131]

After their arrival in Belfast, Congleton and Fishbourne wasted no time travelling to Glenavy to investigate. They spoke to John Larmour, owner of the Glenavy Mills, who confirmed that he stood sponsor at Laura's baptism. Lord Congleton then went to inspect the old church on the banks of Lough Neagh, in the guise of an anonymous gentleman. He struck up a conversation with Lanky Shane, the village sexton, who unsuspectingly showed him the church register. We do not know what, if anything, Lord Congleton found in the register, as the relevant entries do not appear to have survived. Possibly the locals told the two sleuths of the Ram's Island Incident, which was still gossiped about. More likely, from an analysis of the recorded births of Laura's half-brothers and half-sisters they discovered that Laura Bell's parents were never married and that Laura Jane Seymour was not Robert Bell's second wife. The end result of these investigations seems to have been that Laura was ejected from the circle of the Welbeck Street Brethren.[132] Although this was a great setback, Laura had none-theless made friends with some important members of the group who stood by her, including Lord Ward (later the 1st Earl Dudley), and her position in society was sufficiently secure to continue her religious crusade. This was greatly assisted by Elizabeth, Dowager Duchess of Gordon, whose support enabled Laura to ignore those who plotted her downfall. Elizabeth Gordon (1794-1864), after a lifetime of earnest devotion and Christian undertakings, was regarded as the foremost evangelical patron in Scotland and her support enabled the return of Mrs Thistlethwayte to the upper strata of London society.

MUSIC AND LYRICS

There is some evidence, in addition to the *Ram's Island* book previously mentioned, that Laura Thistlethwayte may have published both music and lyrics. The *National Union Catalog* under the reference 'Thistlethwayte, Laura Eliza Jane Seymour (Bell)' has the entry 'see Laura Bell'.[133] Unfortunately the Laura Bell entries do not cross-reference back to Thistlethwayte, and they are all sheet music. Some 'Laura Bell' items have lyrics which include American colloquial expressions, and would never have been written by a fervent Victorian preacher. The most likely item of interest is *Go Beautiful and Gentle Dove*, words by the Rev. W.L. Bowles, the music composed by 'Mrs. Thistlethwayte' (New York, published by James L. Hewitt & Co.), undated, but from the late nineteenth century. The song *Farewell! if ever fondest prayer*, text by George Gordon Noel Byron, Lord Byron (1788-1824), was also apparently set to music by a 'Mrs. Thistlethwayte'[134] but there is no direct evidence to link Laura to any of the music and it is not impossible that both were actually by Laura's mother-in-law.

15 GROSVENOR SQUARE

The building numbered 15-16 Grosvenor Square had been taken over by property speculator Kensington Lewis in 1847, and split into two houses. Having spent some £5,000 on alterations, including the addition of a rear wing to No. 15, he soon leased No. 16 in 1848. But No. 15, because of its bad structural problems, was unoccupied until 1856 when the Thistlethwaytes moved in. Indeed when Laura finally left the house over thirty years later the subsequent tenant had to spend a substantial amount on structural repairs before he could move in.[135] This problem may well have enabled the Thistlethwaytes to live at such a prestigious address at a lower rent than the norm.

The 1881 Census of England provides an interesting snapshot of life in Grosvenor Square. Laura is described as head of the household and there is no mention of her husband, Frederick, who was staying at the Inveran Hotel, Criech, in Scotland on the day of the census. The house at 15 Grosvenor Square was maintained by no fewer than eighteen staff — a housekeeper, two lady's maids, three housemaids, two laundrymaids, two kitchenmaids, a laundress, steward, two footmen, a coachman, groom and two stablemen. There is no mention of a cook, who must have been elsewhere on the day the census took place. Of the thirteen houses adjacent to the Thistlethwaytes in Grosvenor Square only four had the head of the house in residence, the rest being inhabited by a few servants who maintained the house while the families were away. Of these homes where the head of the house was in residence the husband and wife at No. 8 had only eight servants, No. 17 (husband, wife, two daughters) had nineteen servants including a Swiss governess, and No. 19b (husband, wife, two sons) seven servants. The Thistlethwaytes would therefore seem to have employed a surfeit of domestic staff and servants that were apparently required to maintain just a childless middle-aged couple one of whom entertained.

During their occupancy, the other residents of Grosvenor Square were an endless succession of Dukes, Viscounts, Earls and Knights. Of particular note was No. 9 Grosvenor Square, occupied in 1856-63 by Allen Alexander Bathurst, later 6th Earl Bathurst (and thus a relative of Laura's husband) and Baron Dufferin & Claneboye (later 1st Marquess of Dufferin and Ava) who also lived at No. 9 from 1866 to 1872. Lord Dufferin was at this time well on his way to becoming the greatest ambassadorial diplomat to come out of Ulster, soon to be Governor-General of Canada and eventually to become Viceroy of India.

While living at Grosvenor Square Frederick Thistlethwayte pursued his life as a Victorian gentleman, the highlight of the year being seasonal visits to his hunting lodge in Scotland for the shoot. It is unclear whether or how long after her marriage Laura continued her career of prostitution with the wealthiest of lovers, but a belief in its continuation was widespread at this time. Among her reputed lovers were the artists Buckner and Clayton, both of whom painted her portrait. It was further alleged Laura

69

had been Landseer's mistress[136] and helped him sculpt one of the lions now standing round Nelson's Column in Trafalgar Square. Such a studied pronouncement on her relationship to the artist Sir Edwin Landseer, by the Gladstone family archivist A.T. Bassett, is the strongest claim we have that Laura continued to have *affaires* after she and her husband settled down in 15 Grosvenor Square. It is supported by the comment of 6 January 1864 when Gladstone wrote to Laura informing her that the Royal Academy artist J.R. Herbert had spoken to him regarding her relationship with Landseer.[137] Herbert (1810-90), who as a painter was best known for his religious subjects, was not only a friend of Prime Minister Gladstone but also a close friend of Landseer, his neighbour and billiards partner. One is tempted to imagine the effect on the viewer of introducing Laura into the popular print of Landseer as the great artist alone at work with his lions (Plate 10). Furthermore, this accomplishment of artistic endeavour is not as far-fetched as first appears. In 1875 Laura sculpted a bust of William Gladstone, who showed a photograph of it to his wife.[138] The Gladstones purchased the bust, but sadly it can no longer be identified. This achievement raises the fascinating possibility of the existence of other unrecognised pieces of sculpture by Mrs Thistlethwayte.

In parallel with her evangelical preaching, and in the long term a much more successful occupation from all aspects, were the teas, luncheons and dinners at 15 Grosvenor Square where Laura Thistlethwayte entertained. They were in many ways her greatest achievement, enabling her to be the centre of attention for, and potentially an influence upon, some of the leading statesmen of the day. In the household she was clearly the prime mover and organiser of these events, and Frederick's participation in them seems at best somewhat limited.

It is difficult to obtain an accurate indication of life in Grosvenor Square and the relationship between Mr and Mrs Thistlethwayte.

Plate 10. *Landseer sculpting the Trafalgar Square lions*

Many years later Carew Hazlitt recalled:

> It was a singular household. Thistlethwaite [sic] and his
> wife, a very pretty little woman, did not see much company,
> and did not agree very well. Every evening there was a sort
> of state dinner at eight, and a costly dessert, and only those
> two, one at one extremity of a long table, and the other at
> the other.[139]

The author of *More Uncensored Recollections* recalled that when
no longer in her youth Laura was still more than capable of dealing
with gentlemen:

> The only two Magdalens of any real importance in England
> were Anonyma, the first wife of Charlie Rivers Wilson,
> and Laura Bell, who became Mrs. Thistlethwaite [sic]. Of
> course, I knew neither of these ladies in their youth, but,
> even in their autumn, they were both very charming, and the
> last named still retained the beautiful shoulders for which in
> her springtide, she had been famous. And these shoulders
> were useful to her even in her maturity, as I will narrate. I
> had been lunching at her house in Grosvenor Square, and
> the atmosphere was one of the most intense respectability. It
> was a very hot day in June, and Mrs. Thistlethwaite had on a
> dress which showed the famous and still beautiful shoulders.
> She asked me if I thought Sam Lewis would let her have
> some money to help a friend, and I looked at the historic
> shoulders and said 'Yes, Mrs. Thistlethwaite, I'm certain he
> will if you will only go dressed as you are now.' She smiled:
> understood and took my advice. Sam saw the shoulders and
> signed the cheque. He liked to look at beautiful things, even
> if he could never hope to possess them.[140]

According to Holden, on being shown into Laura's draw-ing room one afternoon Lord Shaftesbury was astounded to encounter the scene of an eminent statesman on his knees in front of his hostess in an attitude of devotion as a practical joke.[141] Plate 11, taken from a photographic carte-de-visite, shows Laura in her later years. Henry Coke, in his *Tracks of a Rolling Stone*, provided the following recollection:

> Her Irish wit and sparkling merriment, her cajolery, her good nature and feminine artifice, were attractions which, in the eyes of the male sex, fully atoned for her youthful indiscretions.
>
> My intimacy with both Mr. and Mrs. Thistlethwayte extended over many years; and it is but justice to her memory to aver that, to the best of my belief, no wife was ever more faithful to her husband.[142]

One of the more interesting families in Laura's close circle of friends was the Pelham-Clintons. As previously mentioned, Lord Lincoln (Henry Pelham Finnes Pelham-Clinton) is believed to have become acquainted with Laura in Dublin during the mid-1840s, where as Chief Secretary he was the most likely can-didate as Laura's lover who told her the political secrets of Dublin Castle. He succeeded his father as the 5th Duke of Newcastle-under-Lyme in 1851, and is nowadays remembered as the unfor-tunate Secretary of State for War during the first few years of the Crimean War, and for his even more unfortunate and scandalous divorce.[143]

In 1847 Susan, Lord Lincoln's wife, abandoned her husband and children and ran away to the continent with Lord Walpole. The result of the ensuing scandal was a pregnancy and the birth of one Horatio Walpole. Before the birth William Gladstone was sent to visit her to seek a reconciliation between husband and

73

Plate 11. *Laura Thistlethwayte's carte-de-visite*

wife, but she refused admittance to her villa claiming ill health. Divorce proceedings by Lord Lincoln ensued on the grounds of adultery by Lady Lincoln which was subsequently proved in both the Ecclesiastical Court and the House of Lords. Lord Lincoln's health was greatly affected by the scandal and dissolution of his marriage, and there is a widespread belief that the resulting stress contributed to his early death in 1864 aged fifty-two.

Shortly afterwards, in 1865, we have one of the first mentions of Laura Thistlethwayte in the *Gladstone Diaries*, when she and Gladstone spoke of the death of the 5th Duke of Newcastle.[144] Further evidence of Laura's friendship with the Duke was forthcoming when the eminent banker Lord Kinnaird (executor of Newcastle's will) discovered amongst the Duke's papers 'many really touching and apparently devotional epistles penned by her'.[145]

While in Naples in 1862, Lady Susan Lincoln had married her Belgian courier, Jean Alexis Opdebeck, but by the 1880s she had returned to England. In 1885 Lady Susan Opdebeck was living in very reduced circumstances and in need of financial assistance, so she wrote to both Laura and William Gladstone to ask for support in her attempt to obtain some money from her grandson, now the 7th Duke of Newcastle. Gladstone wrote to Laura that he was 'sorry for Lady Susan, but you have done all you can'.[146] Regarding the death of a penniless Lady Susan in 1889, Gladstone commented to Laura that she could 'look back on a series of most kind acts' towards her.[147] According to Esmore, after the 5th Duke's death:

[Lord Kinnaird] showed himself so confident in the sincere piety of the repentant Mrs. Thistlethwayte that he must needs commit to her care the young Duke of Newcastle. And to such good purpose, too, that for five years or thereabouts, the young nobleman was wont to spend many Wednesday and Saturday evenings at the Thistlethwayte mansion in Grovesnor Square discussing, often until the early morning,

75

knotty points of theology with his charming hostess.[148]

Such earnest religious discussions, if indeed he was the young man concerned, were not a success with young 'Linky' the 6th Duke of Newcastle (Henry Pelham Alexander Clinton), a wastrel whose gambling debts were only paid off by marriage to a wealthy heiress which saved him from ruin. However, Esmore may have confused him with his brother Edward who alone of the 5th Duke's children seems to have inherited the strong sense of duty and Christian outlook of his ancestors. Another brother, Arthur, lived a dissipated life, and the youngest brother, Lord Albert, was also plagued by debt.

Lord Edward Pelham-Clinton embarked on a military career, retiring as Lieutenant Colonel in 1880 in order to advise and direct his nephew, Linky's son, who became the 7th Duke of Newcastle. Lord Edward also took Laura Thistlethwayte under his wing, and in her will she named him as executor and trustee.[149] Furthermore, Lord Edward inherited her personal goods including the portrait of Laura as a child (Plate 3) and on his death the portrait passed to his wife's niece Catherine Matilda Annie Georgina Farnham.[150]

As Mrs Thistlethwayte, Laura clearly did not devote herself solely to the wishes and desires of her husband, but adopted a high profile and independent lifestyle. Frederick Thistlethwayte was unable to cap Laura's extravagant spending on lavish clothes, and claimed that in at least one instance the guests at 15 Grosvenor Square were there at his wife's invitation, not his, and that he asked them all to leave.[151] Those who believed that Laura continued her career as a courtesan after her marriage implied that any gentleman she invited to visit her was, or had once been, her lover. Regularly entertaining very eminent persons at dinner parties at their home in 15 Grosvenor Square when her husband was not present, she certainly left herself open to speculation concerning the closeness of her relationship with her guests. Henry Coke reminisced:

The last time I met Mr. Gladstone there [15 Grosvenor Square] the Duke of Devonshire and Sir W. Harcourt were both present. I once dined with Mrs. Thistlethwayte in the absence of her husband, when the only others were Munro of Novar — the friend of Turner, and the envied possessor of a splendid gallery of his pictures — and the Duke of Newcastle — then a Cabinet Minister. Such were the notabilities whom the famous beauty gathered about her.[152]

Over many years a remarkable list of men sat round the Thistlethwayte table to discuss politics and religion, and an invitation to No. 15 Grosvenor Square was regarded as one of the smartest invitations one could receive. Ex-lovers and admirers from the olden days traded their wit and wisdom with the most distinguished gentlemen including the likes of Sir William Harcourt, A.W. Kinglake (the eminent historian of the Crimean War and travel writer), Charles Villiers (Liberal MP), Lord Roseberry (MP, member of the Privy Council, fellow of the Royal Society), John Delane (editor of *The Times* for thirty-six years), Abraham Hayward (essayist and teller of anecdotes), Madamme Novikoff (who campaigned on behalf of Russia), Lord Torrington, Sir Alexander Cockburn (the Lord Chief Justice of England), the Duke of Devonshire (Irish Secretary and Secretary for War), Munro of Novar (sculptor and friend of Turner), the painter J. R. Herbert, Sir Fitzroy Kelly (Solicitor General and Lord Chief Baron of the Exchequer) and many others.

For political heavyweights such as these to have regularly dined at 15 Grosvenor Square over many years says much for the abilities of the hostess. Although throughout this period 'The Irish Question' was a key political debate, and one upon which Laura would no doubt have made her opinion known, these evenings must have had a much wider political influence upon the participants which has yet to be considered by historians.

But the most famous and eminent of these guests, and by far the most enigmatic, was the Prime Minister, the Right Honourable William Ewart Gladstone.

5

THE PRIME MINISTER'S 'DEAR SPIRIT'
1864-1894

a ring is a band, and in it I will have
engraved 'L.T. to W.E.G.'
　　　　　　—William Gladstone

Laura Bell's relationship with William Ewart Gladstone was the most important of her life, and the most difficult to assess. The official view seems to be that it was a platonic friendship and almost all one-sided. Biographies of Gladstone mention neither their closeness nor her influence on him. The defence of Gladstone's morals and a reticence to contemplate their relationship were strictly maintained by biographers for many years after Gladstone's death. The publication of the *Gladstone Diaries* (the last volume of which appeared in 1994) documented for the first time the frequency of their communications and gave clear, if limited, evidence as to the scope of their involvement.

William Ewart Gladstone was the most eminent Victorian statesman, being regarded by many as the the dominant political figure of his generation. He was Prime Minister four times between 1868 and 1894 and is remembered as a great orator, active legislator and reformer, a Liberal with a deeply religious outlook and a highly moralistic tone which represented the best qualities of Victorian England. Gladstone's third and fourth ministries were dominated by his advocacy of home rule for Ireland and both came to a premature end with defeats of Home Rule bills in the Commons and House of Lords respectively. Even when he was out of office he continued to crusade for home rule. Given Laura's origins and background it would be surprising if she did not make known to Gladstone her views concerning the political situation on the Emerald Isle. There is much work for future historians seeking to uncover the true influence of Laura Bell and her political dinners upon the Prime Minister and his policies.

The published evidence of the relationship between Laura Thistlethwayte and William Gladstone resides in the 14-volume *Gladstone Diaries*. Laura is mentioned over one thousand times in the diaries between 1864 and 1894. Unfortunately these diaries are not a literary account but, rather, comprise a list of people Gladstone wrote to and saw each day, with an occasional and often cryptic comment after a name. Three ways in which Laura is mentioned are (i) that he wrote to her, (ii) that he saw her, i.e. that they met socially, and (iii) that he had luncheon or dinner with her (Fig. 3). During the nine years after 1868 Laura is mentioned on average more than once per week, the peak being some 89 times in 1870 which comprised writing to her 64 times, seeing her 20 times and dining with her 5 times. From 1878 the annual count gradually declines from 38 to just 9 mentions in 1893, the last full year before her death.

Because of her scandalous past and somewhat inappropriate relationship with him, Gladstone uniquely in the diary always referred to her as 'Mrs. Th.' (not Thistlethwayte) and her home as '15 G.S.' (not Grosvenor Square). Furthermore their letters were exchanged by private means, and not by the usual civil service courier system. An 'X' sometimes appeared against her name in the diaries, the symbol indicating rescue work — Gladsone's attempt to save individual prostitutes from a life of degradation — but in at least some cases this refers to both of them helping other women.

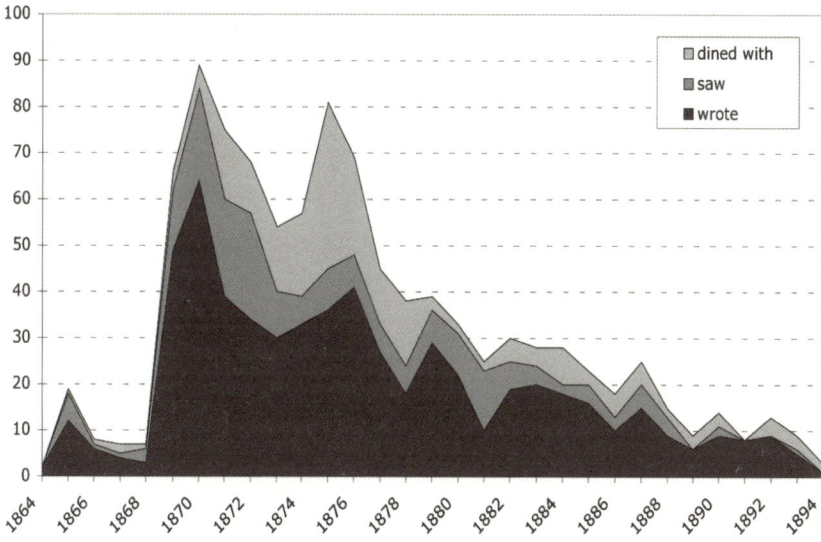

Fig. 3. *Gladstone Diaries — mentions of Laura Thistlethwayte*

The first mention of Laura Thistlethwayte in the *Gladstone Diaries* was on 10 December 1864. At the time Laura was in her early thirties and Gladstone (Plate 12) was fifty-five years of age. This was followed up with a diary entry early in 1865 concerning a long talk between them occasioned by the death of a mutual friend, the Duke of Newcastle. Soon they were writing to each other regularly, occasionally meeting at Grosvenor Square either at Mrs Thistlethwayte's religious luncheons or for dinner in the evening with a small and select group of politicians and influential figures. There is no evidence Mrs Gladstone was ever invited, and indeed she appears to have been formally introduced to Laura for the first time many years later in 1887.[153] This sequence of letters and meetings continued constantly for almost thirty years, being punctuated by great crises induced by conscience or fear of rejection by society which from time to time engulfed Laura. Her surviving letters to Gladstone, never dated, shriek of passion and religious mania, but contain little of interest. Many of them are written on notepaper with a curious mystical image for a letterhead. But any interpretation of the surviving letters must be tempered by the fact that much of the correspondence was systematically destroyed and the remaining examples were presumably deemed safe for suitable persons to read.

As their relationship developed, so did the way Gladstone addressed Laura in his correspondence — from a conventional 'Mrs. Thistlethwayte' (August 1869) to 'Dear Wounded Spirit' and 'Dear Spirit' (October 1869) before returning to 'Mrs. Thistlethwayte' in 1879. Gladstone signed his letters with only his initials 'WEG'. Plate 13 reproduces part of a typical letter from Gladstone (dated 16 March 1871), to which has been added a comment by Laura. It illustrates the difficulty in deciphering the holograph, particularly that of Laura, whose calligraphy gushes emotion and energy but not clarity. The text reads as follows:

Plate 12. *W.E. Gladstone, c.1860*

[I go out of] town till Monday, & on Sunday again to Windsor! So go the ſtars! Nevertheless I have an idea that on Saturday if we have juſt a Cabinet I may get to G. Square either at two when you will probably have luncheon or else at five for a half hour.

God Bless You

Ever yours   WEG

I return the Petrarchs. You ought not lightly to flirt with them.

Susceptible was meant to be general, not special as you suppose &, as general, it is true.

and at the end of the letter Mrs Thiſtlethwayte appended the comments:

These firſt words of welcome being the only kindness received by me for nearly a year oh! what I have suffered Thank God I can never again suffer as I have done. Will he bear with my weakness — God willing I hope to get ſtrong.

He can care for nothing of mine. or nothing from me. oh how madly I love

March 16th [154]

The few insights the *Gladſtone Diaries* and Gladſtone-Thiſtleth-wayte correspondence provide are in the main fruſtratingly banal or cryptic, although further research on their contents might well prove fruitful. On the whole the correspondence reflects the art of Victorian letter-writing, letting each other see letters from third parties (Lord Carysfort to Laura,[155] which Gladſtone then de-ſtroyed as requeſted),[156] thanks passed on for gifts (Lady A. Ewing thanking Laura via Gladſtone),[157] condolences on the death of friends (Lord Annesley, whose death caused Laura vivid recollec-

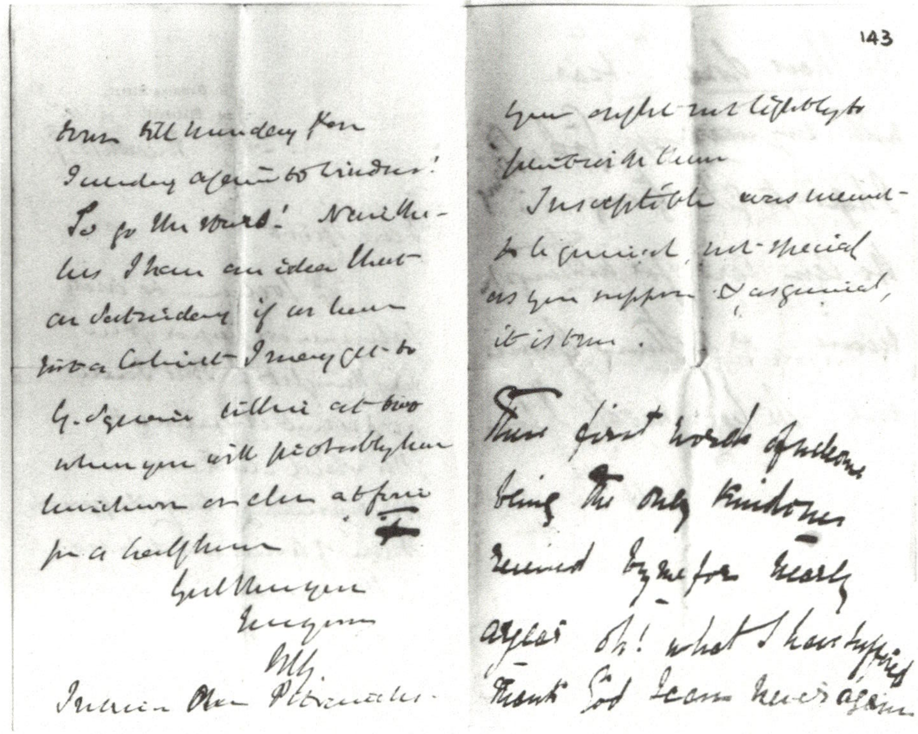

Plate 13. *Letter from W.E. Gladstone to Laura with her comments, 1871*

tions),[158] endless mentions of illness and health, lending each other books of a religious nature, thanks from Mrs Gladstone via her husband for Mr Thistlethwayte's gift of salmon and venison from his hunting lodge in Scotland, and so on. The impression given is that on Laura's side the surviving letters reflect an obsessive and agitated woman who, owing to her impulsive nature, showered Gladstone with expensive gifts which he was forever seeking to return but he was unable to do so, not wishing to give offence or catastrophically cause a break-up of their relationship.

One evening in July 1869, while he was dining at 15 Grosvenor Square, Laura promised Gladstone she would write her personal history,[159] and over the next few months it was delivered to him in at least twenty-three fascicles.[160] He was clearly affected by the tale of her youth, but other than deeply expressed sentiment his subsequent letters to Laura which have survived provide little factual information when referring to her story. Concerning sections XIV-XVII of the story (relating to her time in Belfast) Gladstone commented that the tale had only got as far as her fourteenth year,[161] indicating how much significance Laura ascribed to retelling the story of her childhood. It is no coincidence that this period of 1869-70 provides the maximum number of mentions of Laura in the *Gladstone Diaries*, and her manuscript autobiography undoubtedly provided sufficient evidence to enable Gladstone to develop his relationship with, and championing of, Laura for the rest of her life. Gladstone returned the manuscript to Laura in February 1893,[162] less than two years before her death, but it has since disappeared and is presumed destroyed. From the time she arrived in London in the late 1840s Laura also kept a diary,[163] but again its present whereabouts are unknown.

It is clear from an analysis of the *Gladstone Diaries* that at one time Laura Thistlethwayte meant much more to Gladstone than a mere acquaintance or lady friend. In October 1869 Laura gave Gladstone a ring, and he proposed it be engraved with both their initials, informing Laura of his perilous decision that 'a ring is a band and in it I will have engraved L.T. to W.E.G.'.[164] Common sense prevailed however, although the ring was inscribed with the single initial 'L'.[165] The ring was prominently displayed on his hand and Gladstone (who had already informed his wife) was soon questioned about it by at least two friends.[166]

Several times the *Gladstone Diaries* mention that after dining with Laura at 15 Grosvenor Square, Gladstone would accompany her to the theatre to see a play of her choice. The relationship developed, and during the first half of 1875 Gladstone visited Laura for luncheon and dinner an average of twice per week. A crisis occurred in October 1875, as a result of which they both spent a weekend at Cirencester, the home of Lord Bathurst. This permitted Gladstone three lengthy 'visits' (i.e. private meetings) with Laura that gave him much food for thought.[167] Lord Bathurst was a Thistlethwayte relative, the only one Laura seems to have become attached to. He is mentioned as frequently as anyone in the surviving correspondence, and Laura gave Gladstone a touching account of his death in 1878.[168]

Outsiders acknowledged the singular relationship between Laura Thistlethwayte and Gladstone, but were diffident in defining its scope and nature. On 23 March 1887 the poet Robert Browning told Lady Layard that when he had recently gone to dine with the Ponsonby sisters he had been annoyed to find that Laura Thistlethwayte was there because it was actually a party for Gladstone.[169] Lady St Helier was not completely convinced that it was a platonic relationship and wrote of Gladstone:

For many years he was a frequent guest at the house of Mrs Thistlethwaite [sic], who in her later life became an evangelist of the most developed type. In that respect he was not singular, because her society was much frequented by other men who also occupied prominent social positions.

Her great beauty, her plausibility, and — to Mr. Gladstone
— her apparently intense sincerity in the religious beliefs
which she held, appealed most strongly to him.[170]

Another recollection of Laura's entertaining was also less than
wholehearted in its praise:

> She had many friends, and some of her methods of keeping
> them up to the mark were original. Eventually she turned
> very religious, and held Friday and Sunday teas, when she
> discussed religion and kisses with her friends.
>
> Mr. Gladstone was an admirer of hers, and liked to discuss
> with her ecclesiastical dogma. Being a High Churchman,
> he fasted on Fridays and had a fish luncheon, after which it
> was his habit to attend Mrs. Thistlethwaite's tea-party and
> receive the kiss of peace.[171]

The dual use of the word 'kiss' and its implications would not
have gone unnoticed by readers of the above recollections. Henry
Coke, who had known Frederick Thistlethwayte since boyhood,
went even further, writing:

> at my friend's [Frederick Thistlethwayte's] house in
> Grosvenor Square I used frequently to meet Mr. Gladstone,
> sometimes alone, sometimes at dinner.[172]

Again the use of the word 'alone' would have expressed much to
the reader.

DEBTS AND COURT CASES

Laura's reckless spending periodically caused financial difficulties
in the Thistlethwaite household, to the extent that on several occasions Frederick publicly disowned his wife's debts. The relationship

between the Thistlethwaytes in later married life is characterised by a series of court cases caused by Laura's spending spiralling out of control, and her husband Frederick's refusal to pay her debts.

In 1870, and in debt for an amazing £25,000, Laura was forced to sign a written contract for her husband undertaking not to amass any more debts and agreeing to live within the means of her allowance.[173] Around this time the relationship between husband and wife reached its nadir, and there was talk of a separation.[174] The downfall of many a courtesan, the ability to spend money more quickly than they could obtain it, was an addiction Laura was never able to overcome. In 1878 Frederick was compelled to order the issue of a public notice to her tradesmen creditors to the effect that his wife had no authority to purchase items using her husband's name as credit.[175]

Laura continued to amass debts, the tradesmen assuming that Mr Thistlethwayte would rather pay up than risk the embarrassment of a court case. But Frederick called their bluff and refused to pay his wife's debts. Not surprisingly an action was brought against him shortly afterwards by a Mr Aaron Schwaebe, owner of the West End milliners Madame Rosalie, over an unpaid bill for £1,000.[176]

In court Laura Thistlethwayte claimed her annual dress allowance of £500 was altogether inadequate for her lifestyle and that she needed to dress elegantly (and by implication expensively) in order to receive at dinner men of rank and fashion. Her husband stated that his own wish was that she dress in a much more quiet and humble (and thus much less expensive) fashion. Furthermore he stated that these fashionable and important men were invited to dine at 15 Grosvenor Square only at his wife's, and definitely not at his own, invitation. Lord Coleridge awarded the judgement and costs to Frederick Thistlethwayte. Tradesmen might have been expected to learn from the case, but this was not so. In 1881 another tradesman took Frederick to court for his wife's debts, but the result was yet again a successful outcome for the husband.[177]

The most serious example of Laura's profligacy was the Padwick-Thistlethwayte suit for debts in 1879. Once again Frederick seems to have refused to acknowledge a debt, caused by Laura's borrowing money on account of her husband's illness.[178]

Henry Padwick was a well-known moneylender, of whom Julian Osgood Field said 'mendacity winked at you from every crease and wrinkle in his face'.[179] Padwick's strategy was to threaten to call as witnesses the guests Laura entertained at 15 Grosvenor Square, his star witness being no other than William Gladstone. Frederick Thistlethwayte wrote to Gladstone apologising for the subpoena[180] but stated he had no intention of settling the case.[181] A few days later a disconcerted Laura sent a further apology.[182] Frederick once again denied being a party to the visit of these guests, forcing Gladstone to write to Laura warning that the Thistlethwaytes' reputation had suffered in the previous trial[183] and this case would drive her friends from the door.[184] To help the Thistlethwaytes financially, Gladstone returned gifts Laura had given him, which cost hundreds of pounds.[185] Laura also informed Gladstone that she resolutely refused three offers to pay Padwick from her friends.[186] To the relief of all concerned the case seems to have been resolved before it came to court.

On 7 August 1887 Frederick Thistlethwayte passed away. As with every other aspect of Laura's life, her husband's death was neither a natural nor a straightforward event. A succinct account of the tragedy was published in the pages of the *Morning Post*:

We have to record the death on Sunday night from a fatal accident of Augustus Frederick Thistlethwayte at his residence in Grosvenor Square. It appears that Mr. Thistlethwayte was in the habit of keeping a loaded revolver on a table by his bedside, and that being seized with a fainting fit, he had stumbled against the table, knocking down the pistol and causing it to explode with fatal result to himself.[187]

This convenient if totally unconvincing explanation enabled the decision to be taken that no potentially embarrassing inquest was necessary. Unsurprisingly rumours soon circulated that this conclusion was not the correct one, and even Gladstone noted in his diary that he was only completely persuaded that it was an accident after a discussion with Mrs Thistlethwayte a fortnight later.[188] It was reported that the revolver on the bedside table was sometimes used to summon the servants[189] and rather surprisingly this may have had a basis in reality. Laura's nephew Robert John Bell on a visit from the United States in the 1860s commented in his diary that 15 Grosvenor Square had 'servants everywhere … the house was full of sterling silver and the ceilings full of holes'.[190]

A newspaper obituary summarised Frederick's character from the distance of a Scottish viewpoint thus:

Mr. Thistlethwayte was a man of high character and deeply religious convictions. He took a great interest in all religious movements, and at one time it was no uncommon thing to see him in Hyde Park on Sunday afternoons addressing large crowds. He had a marvellous knowledge of the Scriptures and being endowed with a wonderful memory, could without reference to the Book quote long passages … He will be much missed in Lochaber, where he made his home for so many years, where he gave employment to a very large number of people, and where his innumerable acts of kindness caused him to be greatly endeared.[191]

Frederick was a shadowy figure in our story, in his youth making a reckless and foolish marriage when he came into wealth, which was then squandered by a vain and spendthrift wife whom he several times disowned in public when her debts became too unmanageable. He seems to have been a religious man, or at least deeply Christian in outlook, yet his only passion seems to have been deer hunting and salmon fishing from his lodge in Scotland. He left a personal estate of £71,561-1-4, and the will was administered by Lieutenant Colonel Edward Henry Trafalgar Digby (39 Belgrave Square) and the Reverend Frederick John Ponsonby (3 Cambridge Place, Regent's Park).

WOODBINE COTTAGE

As a widow, Laura Thistlethwayte slipped quietly into obscurity and out of fame, leaving Grosvenor Square and moving to Woodbine Cottage, West End Road, Hampstead — a house with a large garden and paddock. As an elderly widow she lived a quiet life, her only noteworthy actions apparently being a connection with many local charities and in particular the Society for the Prevention of Cruelty to Animals. By this time Gladstone's relationship with her had long since become a duty on him rather than a close friendship. A couple of months before her husband Frederick's death in 1887 Laura had visited Pevers Cottage, where she unexpectedly encountered Gladstone and his wife Catherine, to whom she was introduced for the first time.[192] The last few mentions of Laura in the *Gladstone Diaries* are when William and Catherine Gladstone stopped off at Woodbine Cottage for afternoon tea.[193] On 17 May 1894 Gladstone drove to Hampstead for the last time, to visit Laura who was then in ill health. She died at Woodbine Cottage on 30 May. Due to eyesight problems Gladstone had stopped regular entries in his diary a week earlier and so he left no obituary note, no final insight into his enigmatic relationship with Laura Thistlethwayte.

In 1896 Gladstone, conscious of his own mortality, made a formal declaration on his marital fidelity. In this very carefully worded document for posterity he declared that had never been guilty of 'infidelity to the marriage bed'[194] but the statement was so limited in scope that as potential legal evidence in the Wright vs. Gladstone libel case in 1927 it was considered worthless and was in fact a liability.[195] In *Portraits and Criticisms* (1927) Captain Peter E. Wright claimed that William Gladstone had affairs with unnamed ladies. William was long since dead and so his son Herbert Gladstone provoked Wright to sue him for libel. During the trial, in February 1927, the relationship between Laura Bell (among others) and Gladstone was discussed in court. Herbert Gladstone's defence team refused to offer as evidence the *Gladstone Diaries*, surviving Gladstone-Thistlethwayte correspondence, or Gladstone's sworn declaration of marital fidelity, for fear they would exonerate Captain Wright. The jury found Herbert Gladstone not guilty, vindicated his father's high moral character, and Peter Wright had to apologise to all concerned for *Portraits and Criticisms*. By the time of Laura's death in the summer of 1894 the scandal and fame of her early years had faded into history, and in any case it was not the sort of thing that one spoke of in late Victorian society. A typical bowdlerized obituary read as follows:

A familiar and once well-known lady passed away last week at her residence in Hampstead. Mrs. Thistlethwayte's name does not convey very much to the present younger generation; but to those whose memories carry them back for thirty years no name was better known, and no hospitality was more munificently dispensed than that of Mr. and Mrs. Frederick Thistlethwayte, both in Grosvenor Square and in the Scotch home where they always went for the shooting season. For many years past Mrs. Thistlethwayte devoted herself to good works, and no one who ever heard her preach will be likely to forget how impressive and eloquent she was. Since her husband's death, Mrs. Thistlethwayte nearly always resided at her lovely suburban home, Woodbine Cottage, Hampstead; where, when she felt strong enough, she received a large circle of friends. A very clever woman, with a wonderful flow of conversation, she had to the laſt the power of attraċting clever men of the day. Mr. Gladſtone was one of her greateſt admirers, and he and Mrs. Gladſtone passed a good deal of their time at Woodbine Cottage of late years. Mrs. Thiſtlethwayte declined to increase her circle, although many were anxious to be included in it who undoubtedly might be called brilliant and exclusive. She was a beautiful woman with a diſtinċt personality.[196]

The *World* was able to publish the following surprisingly malevolent and prudish yet at the same time praiseworthy obituary of Laura:

Mrs. Thiſtlethwayte, who died laſt week at her pretty Woodbine Cottage in Fortune Green Lane, will be recognised, but only by the very elderly, through her four baptismal names, 'Laura Eliza Jane Seymour', as the once notorious and beautiful 'Laura Bell'. That name was coupled (with cauſtic candour) by the ſtreet ballad-mongers of the early fifties with that of the handsome young Nepaulese Prince Jung Bahadur. The young woman's portrait was in all the shops, her sayings, and, ſtill more, her doings, in everybody's mouth. After a few seasons, a wealthy young masher thought fit to amuse the town by marrying Miss Bell, who, as Mrs. Thiſtlethwayte, played the part of Maddalena Penitente very prettily, preaching, diſtributing traċts in the parks, leċturing to young girls at Craven Chapel and to the young shopmen of large firms — when the principals would admit so elegantly dressed a preacher.

After the tragical death, by accident, of her husband in Grosvenor Square, Mrs. Thiſtlethwayte retired to her Hampſtead cottage, where, like Handel's Theodora, 'clad in robes of virgin white', she might be seen going to and

94

fro, active at the adjacent church and schools, engaged in good works, and where her presence will be much missed. She had completely realised the possibility of woman equally with man, rising on stepping-stones of a dead self to higher things, and of living down an unenviable reputation. Statesmen were chronicled as being her dinner guests at Woodbine Cottage, and ladies as accompanying them; and though not perhaps *vouée au blanc*, the hostess was partial to a white satin dinner-gown despite advancing years and wrinkles. Mrs. Thistlethwayte's near neighbours, Sir Charles Frazer and Captain Notman, will be concerned at the probable future of her well-kept house and grounds, and the fields wherein does grazed.[197]

At Laura's funeral on 4 June 1894 distinguished mourners included the noted Arctic explorer Admiral Sir Edward Inglefield, the Countess of Winchelsea and Nottingham, Lord Edward Pelham-Clinton and the Dowager Lady Harvey.[198] Laura's personal estate at her death was worth £41,577-0-6, a not insignificant amount in late Victorian England. Her executors and trustees were Lord Edward Pelham-Clinton and Charles Innes, an Inverness solicitor.[199] The most striking aspect of the document was her wish that Woodbine Cottage be provided as a retreat for clergymen (of all denominations) but this bequest was never implemented.

For all her faults, Laura Bell was a most remarkable woman, able to infatuate an intriguing list of lovers and live such a scandalous life. Yet when she became deeply religious and gave up the old ways she was able, over a period of several decades, to assemble round her dinner table some of the most distinguished and intelligent members of Victorian society and eminent men in public life. Until proof positive of her marriage infidelity is uncovered we can only speculate on the truth of the rumours and oblique references that hint at scandal. Many aspects of her tale in this monograph, rather than making a definitive statement, in fact raise many further questions rather than providing answers. If anyone deserved the epitaph 'an enigma wrapped in a mystery' then Laura Bell was that person.

At the end of the story we are left with one final puzzle. Laura was buried in a grave by herself in Paddington Cemetery, although her remains were later transferred to the Thistlethwayte family vault there.[200] Isaac W. Ward (writing as Belfastiensis in 1903) informs us that when Mrs Thistlethwayte died, by her own directions the name engraved on her coffin plate was Laura Jane Seymour — the name she used as a courtesan when she first arrived in London.[201] If this is an accurate report, and Ward's information is usually more detailed and dependable than others, then Laura went to meet her maker recognising neither her unhappy family background nor married life, but as the most famous and remarkable *grande horizontale* of her generation.

Appendix A

THE BELL FAMILY

The genealogical chart in Fig. 2 (see Chapter 1) includes only eleven of the presumed twenty-one siblings: so there are many gaps in our knowledge of Robert Bell and his domestic establishment.

FIRST MARRIAGE

Although nothing is known about Robert Bell's first wife, information about three of the children from this marriage is available :

☞ Anna Maria Bell b. 1815, married John Vernon, son of the Rev. John Vernon of Lisburn, on 30 October 1833. They eventually moved to London (where Laura had been living since 1850) and in the 1860s lived in Frankfort Terrace with their two daughters Louisa (b. c.1846) and Grace (b. c.1851). The Vernons seem to be the only relatives to have kept in touch with Laura, who left her niece Louisa Vernon an annuity — the only member of the extended Bell family to be bequeathed money in Laura's will. The *Belfast Newsletter* of 8 November 1833 records the marriage 'on the 30th ult. in Glenavy Church, Mr John Vernon, eldest son of the Rev. John Vernon, of Lisburn, to Anna Maria, second daughter of Captain Robert Bell, of Bell Brook, Glenavy'. The 1861 Census of England has Annie M. Vernon (widow) and daughters Grace and Louisa living with a governess and servant at Vernon Cottage, Walm Lane, Willesden. In 1871 the family, along with one servant, were sharing 18 Frankfort Terrace Paddington with William Wood, his wife and daughter.

☞ Arthur Wellington Bell (I) b. *c*.1817, d.1837. The *Belfast Newsletter* 6 January 1837 announced: 'At Templemore, on 31ˢᵗ ult. of brain fever, after a few days' illness, Arthur Wellington Bell, medical student, in the 20ᵗʰ year of his age, son of Captain Bell of Glenavy'.

☞ Frederick H. Bell b. *c*.1821, at Bellbrook Co. Dublin, the last son of the first marriage. In the 1840s he emigrated to the United States, where his family included two sons, Robert John and Frank, and a daughter Catherine. Robert John Bell served in the British Army and when in London in the 1860s and 1870s visited 'Aunty Vernon' and his cousins and also several times visited Laura at her house in Grosvenor Square.[202]

No details have survived of the other sons of Robert Bell's first marriage and family tradition has it that they were disinherited by their father because they went to sea.

SECOND MARRIAGE

On 29 August 1822 Robert Bell married Rebecca Bowland in her home town of Arklow County Wicklow. The family was eventually to include the following siblings:

☞ James Bowland Bell b. *c*.1827, d. 1835. The *Belfast Newsletter* 3 April 1835 announced: 'Suddenly, on the 23ʳᵈ ult. at his father's residence, Bell Brook, near Glenavy, James, son of Captain Robert Bell, aged seven years'.

☞ John Bowland Bell b. *c*.1828, d. 1840 aged twelve, the

Belfast Newsletter obituary of 4 January 1841 stating: 'On the 28th ult. John Bowland Bell, aged 12 years, eleventh son of Captain Robert Bell, Bellbrook, Glenavy'.

☞ Robert Henry Bell b. 12 May 1833 at Glenavy to Rebecca and Robert Bell. In 1899 the *Belfast Newsletter* recorded his death, describing him as Robert Bell of Bellbrook, Glenavy, faithful servant to the Waring family for fifty-two years.

☞ James Leonard Bell b. 1 Nov 1835 at Glenavy to Rebecca and Robert Bell (Glenavy Church register).

☞ Arthur Wellington Bell (II) b. 9 Nov 1838 at Glenavy to Rebecca and Robert Bell (Glenavy Church register).

☞ Alicia Seymour Bell b. 4 Aug 1842 at Glenavy to Rebecca and Robert Bell (Glenavy Church register).

The inclusion of the forename Bowland is an example of the tradition often found in Ulster where the second Christian name is the surname of one of the grandparents. Arthur Wellington Bell (II) was the next son to be born after the death of the first son with that name died in December 1836. This older son, who died aged just twenty, must have been especially favoured to have a brother named after him.

Two other daughters of Robert Bell are known. One was recorded in Glenavy Parish Church register as:

☞ Jane Anna n.d. [i.e. natural daughter] of Robert Bell of Bellbrook and Mary Smiley on 25 June 1837.[203]

Although born out of wedlock she was acknowledged as his daughter by Robert Bell. The remaining daughter, for whom no birth or christening details survive, is Laura Eliza Jane Seymour Bell herself.

There are a few other pieces of information relating to the

family that cannot be ascribed to a specific individual or are problematic and contradict other evidence. The family is believed to have comprised some twenty-one sons and daughters (including two illegitimate daughters). According to Esmore there were only three sisters, the eldest sister leading a normal life, settling down and marrying a yeoman farmer from Maralyn. The youngest daughter, on the other hand, tried to follow in Laura's footsteps in the oldest of professions, but was singularly less successful.[204] Horace Wyndham reported that an elder sister named Myra became a much admired actress in the 1860s, although this may have been her stage name.[205] The other person who may well have been a relative was Henry Bell, joint author (with Laura) of *A Short Visit to Ram's Island*. His intimate knowledge of Laura's return visit to Ulster strongly suggests he must have been a close family relative, one she could trust, but other than his address at the Grove Cottage, Near Lambeg, Lisburn, Ireland in September 1853 I have been unable to distinguish him from other contemporary persons of the same name.

Appendix B

A SHORT VISIT TO RAM'S ISLAND
1853

*The Island Queen — an honorary title graciously
bestowed ... by the residents of the neighbourhood*
—Henry Bell

A Short Visit to Ram's Island provides manifest evidence of one
of the stories circulated concerning Laura Bell and yet the little
booklet on closer inspection is both enigmatic and problematical.
The imprint details show the work was printed by A. Welsh of 10
Arthur Square Belfast in 1853 and the three included illustrations
printed by Marcus Ward & Co. of Belfast, one of which is dated
August 1853, confirming the date and place of the incident. Yet
the little volume's physical construction, bibliographical evidence
and censored contents all give rise to further questions.

For a long time only one copy of the booklet was known to
have survived — that in the Linen Hall Library, Belfast. A second
copy has recently come to light in a private library. A careful comparison of both has enabled an initial analysis of the little volume,
the results of which can be seen in Table 1.

The book was printed as a quarto, four pages being printed on
each side of a large sheet of paper which was then folded twice
to give an 8-page gather. Four gathers were printed and bound
together to form the booklet. During the printing of the book

101

pages 15-30 were mistakenly numbered 13-28 giving two page 13s (which were not numbered) and two page 14s (which were numbered). This often encountered typesetting error is usually indicative that the first two gathers of the volume (the first 16 pages) were printed at a different time or in a different press to the last two gathers. Together with the evidence of their typefaces and layout it suggests that the booklet was originally just 16 pages (two gathers), which are reproduced at the end of this Appendix. It comprised the title page and frontispiece, the poem *The Island Queen* with a few notes and a Plate reproducing the sheet music *Bonny Portmore* which was to accompany the lyrics. It is likely that in this first form it was produced around the time of the visit to Ram's Island, although it is unclear whether it was before, during or after the stay. At a later date the final two gathers which comprise the Addenda were printed and bound in with remaining copies of the booklet to form a more substantial item suitable for wider distribution. This is also confirmed in the Addenda itself which begins 'Since compiling the foregoing details, I have been requested by friends to add some further notices of interesting "nooks and corners" in this neighbourhood'. The surviving copies both exhibit the full form of the booklet, and one of them has a presentation date of 1 January 1855, some sixteen months after the events depicted. The inscription date strongly suggests it was a New Year's gift from the author to Sweet Pea rather than that this was the date of publication. This expanded booklet is reminiscent of an example some three years earlier in 1850 when the Marquess of Dufferin and Ava had a similar sized item printed in Belfast for the guests at the 'christening' of Helen's Tower, Clandeboye. In 1861 when the tower was officially opened, remaining copies of the booklet were upgraded with the addition of pages which contained the Tennyson poem *Helen's Tower* and details of the flag raising ceremony, and so it was reissued in an enlarged form to a wider circle of family and friends.

From the comparison of evidence in the two surviving copies of *Ram's Island* documented in Table 1 some conclusions can be deduced. Copy A has no indication of ownership: the only fact relating to its provenance is that it became part of the Linen Hall Library on 18 December 1908 and was rebound in a standard library binding. Copy B has a presentation inscription from the author Henry Bell dated 1 January 1855. Although also rebound, the original plain yellow wrappers have been bound in at the front and back of the volume. In both cases gathers C and D have retained their position bound in before the last leaf of gather B.

The most striking aspect of both copies is that they have almost identical censorship applied where specific printed words have been scraped off the page with a sharp knife and in most cases replaced by a ruled line. The censorship of the two occurrences of the phrase 'Mrs. A.F. Thistlethwayte' replacing it with 'Mrs. A.F. T_____' would make no difference to those who knew the story of Mrs Augustus Frederick Thistlethwayte's visit to Ram's Island. Yet given that this item was privately printed for the author, why did he go to the expense of having it printed and then censoring it himself before issuing it? The change of the phrase 'written and compiled at the particular desire of an esteemed friend' in copy A to '…at the particular desire of esteemed friends' is both subtle and curious, but may provide the answer. The laudatory tone of the work implies the esteemed friend was Laura Bell herself, and that the work was originally produced for Laura to distribute to those who accompanied her during her stay on Ram's Island and to close acquaintances as an amusing keepsake and memento of the reverie.

It therefore appears that the 32-page second version of the booklet was produced for a wider circulation than the original version, and as a consequence required to be censored. This is suggested by the observation that only the original part comprising the first two gathers was censored. It might be supposed in this circumstance that it was essential to be more circumspect, perhaps censoring the arm-in-arm lovers depicted in the woodcut illustration of Ram's Island, or perhaps the use of the phrase 'The Island Queen' might be seen as an insult to the locals in the vicinity of the island, but these aspects remained unchanged. It therefore seems likely that the expurgation of the name Thistlethwayte was to forestall its use as an exhibit in a court of law. As has already been noted the entourage of gamblers, hangers-on and 'languid beauties of the burlesque' who accompanied Laura to Ram's Island were not the sort of people Frederick Thistlethwayte would associate with. This was the period when she was estranged from her husband and and if it was indeed her brother-in-law and not her husband who accompanied her to the island then the motive for the censorship by the author Henry Bell, excising all reference to Thistlethwayte in the booklet, was to forestall its use as evidence in a potential Thistlethwayte divorce case.

The evidence of page mis-numbering and censorship documented in Table 1 is consistent with the 16-page booklet being produced during or shortly after the stay at Ram's Island for those who took part in the visit, and perhaps for a few very close friends of Laura. At a later date the remaining 16 pages were printed so that the combined 32-page booklet could be given wider distribution to friends of the author Henry Bell, after being suitably censored. This scenario would be confirmed by the discovery of a 16-page original booklet without censorship.

Given that I have only been able to locate two copies, it is difficult to determine the reason behind the rarity of this book today. There may have been widespread condemnation of the volume, based upon the recognition of Laura Thistlethwayte, or it may simply be that Henry Bell privately published only a few copies of the book which were then presented to friends and participants in the events. Yet rarely in the history of Victorian printing can such an insignificant and ephemeral item be confirmation of such a spectacular and in many ways unbelievable story of prostitution, high society, religion and politics.

BIBLIOGRAPHICAL DESCRIPTION

Henry Bell : *A Short Visit to Ram's Island*
A. Welsh   Belfast   1853

A SHORT VISIT | TO | Ram's Island, Lough Neagh, | AND ITS VI-CINITY, | IN THE YEAR | MDCCCLIII. | [short rule] | 'Flow, Lagan, flow, along thy banks so green, | Tho' in the system of the world unseen; | Yet dearer to my soul thy waters run, | than all the rills that glide beneath the sun.' | [short rule] | BELFAST: | A. WELSH, 10, ARTHUR-SQUARE. | [short rule] | MDCCCLIII.

Collation: A-D⁴ quarto, 5¼ x 8¼" with gathers C and D sewn between B³ and B⁴

Pagination: (ii), (7) 8-10 (11) 12 (13) 14-28 (13) 14

Contents:

A1ʳᵉᶜᵗᵒ blank

A1ᵛᵉʳˢᵒ frontispiece oval frame of leaves and flowers, hanging from which is a bell with an 'H', inscribed 'M. Ward & Co. Belfast'

A2ʳᵉᶜᵗᵒ title page

A2ᵛᵉʳˢᵒ blank

A3ʳᵉᶜᵗᵒ dedication

A3ᵛᵉʳˢᵒ lithograph *Ram's Island* inscribed 'Henry Bell delt. Aug 1853' and 'Marcus Ward & Co. Lith.'

A4ʳᵉᶜᵗᵒ poem T*he Island Queen*

A4ᵛᵉʳˢᵒ blank

B1ʳᵉᶜᵗᵒ to B2ᵛᵉʳˢᵒ NOTES

B3ʳᵉᶜᵗᵒ to B3ᵛᵉʳˢᵒ POSTSCRIPT

B4ʳᵉᶜᵗᵒ to B4ᵛᵉʳˢᵒ GENTLE READER

C1ʳᵉᶜᵗᵒ to D4ᵛᵉʳˢᵒ ADDENDA

Plate: music of the tune *Bonny Portmore* in a leaf border. Inscribed 'M Ward & Co. Litho 9 Corn Market Belfast', inserted between leaves B3 and C1.

#	Page	Copy A	Copy B	Comments
1	---	Rebound in a library binding	Rebound but with the original plain yellow wrappers bound-in	
2	A1verso	Frontispiece oval of flowers uncoloured	Frontispiece oval of flowers brightly hand-coloured and containing the inscription *Presented to* | *Sweet Pea* | *with Henry Bell's* | *respectful complements* | *1 January 1855* | *Lambeg* | *Lisburn* | *Ireland*	
3	A2recto	Title page – first letter 'r' in 'Arthur Square' broken	Title page – first letter 'r' in 'Arthur Square' broken	Both copies from the same (presumably first and only) issue/edition
4	A3recto	Dedication: ' ... written and compiled at the particular desire of an esteemed friend, _____, for XXXX XX' '	Dedication: ' ... written and compiled at the particular desire of XX esteemed friends _____, for XXXX XX' '	In copy A both the name of the friend and the name after 'for' have been scraped off. Copy B has further been changed from 'an esteemed friend' to 'esteemed friends' to generalise the dedication. What the final removed word was is unclear.
5	A3recto	'this little book. _____ by _____ '	'this little book. _____ by _____ '	Unable to guess the missing words
6	A3verso	Ram's Island lithograph uncoloured	Lithograph coloured in pale blues and browns, gentleman has a blue jacket and brown hat, lady has blue lines on her dress	
7	A4recto	'Mrs. A F T _____'s farewell to Ram's Island'	'Mrs. A F T _____'s farewell to Ram's Island'	The censored word is obviously 'Thistlethwayte'
8	B1recto	'graciously bestowed on Mrs. A F T _____,'	'graciously bestowed on Mrs. A F T _____,'	The censored word is obviously 'Thistlethwayte'
9	B1recto	'skeleton ... measuring in length seven feet'	'skeleton ... measuring in length six XX feet'	Skeleton length changed from seven to six feet
10	B4verso	Notes 'Gentle Reader' ends with printed 'H B'	Below 'H B' it is signed in ink 'Henry Bell'	
11	general	collation A-D4, gathers C and D bound between leaves B3 and B4, page size 5¾ x 8¾ inches, pagination gathers A and B: (1-7) 8-10 (11) 12 (13) 14, pagination gathers C and D:14-28	collation A-D4, gathers C and D bound between leaves B3 and B4, page size 5¾ x 8½ inches, pagination gathers A and B: (1-7) 8-10 (11) 12 (13) 14, pagination gathers C and D:14-28	

Print removed and replaced by ruled line = _____ , print removed and not replaced = XXXX

Table 1. *Analysis of A Short Visit to Ram's Island, 1853*

Plates 14-30.
Facsimile of the first two gathers of the Linen
Hall Library copy of Henry Bell's *A Short Visit
to Ram's Island* (1853), digitised at 600dpi,
reproduced at 85% of original size.

A SHORT VISIT

TO

Ram's Island, Lough Neagh,

AND ITS VICINITY,

IN THE YEAR

MDCCCLIII

'Flow, Lagan, flow, along thy banks so green,
Tho' in the system of the world unseen;
Yet dearer to my soul thy waters run,
Than all the rills that glide beneath the sun.'

BELFAST:
A. WELSH, 10, ARTHUR-SQUARE.

MDCCCLIII.

THE FOLLOWING PAGES,

DESCRIPTIVE OF

SCENERY AND LOCALITIES IN THE NORTH OF IRELAND,

AND

INTERESTING REMINISCENCES CONNECTED THEREWITH,

HAVE BEEN WRITTEN AND COMPILED AT THE PARTICULAR DESIRE OF AN ESTEEMED
FRIEND, ⸺⸺⸺⸺⸺⸺⸺⸺⸺⸺, FOR

𝕿𝖍𝖎𝖘 𝕷𝖎𝖙𝖙𝖑𝖊 𝕭𝖔𝖔𝖐.

⸺⸺⸺⸺, BY ⸺⸺⸺⸺

𝕳𝕰𝕹𝕽𝖄 𝕭𝕰𝕷𝕷.

The Grove Cottage,
Near Lambeg, Lisburn, Ireland.

15th September, 1853.

Ram's Island.

The Island Queen.

MRS. A. F. T_____'S

FAREWELL TO RAM'S ISLAND,

LOUGH NEAGH,

ON THE OCCASION OF HER DEPARTURE FOR HER RESIDENCE IN LONDON,
AFTER HAVING SPENT SOME WEEKS IN LORD O'NEILL'S COTTAGE, ON THE
ISLAND, IN THE AUTUMN OF MDCCCLIII.

Air—'Bonny Portmore.'

FAREWELL Ballinderry, and dear Aghalee,
Ram's Island—its Round Tower, and old Ivy Tree;
I'll remember you oft, with a heart running o'er,
Sandy Bay, and Shane's Castle, and Bonny Portmore.
  In absence, kind fancy, these scenes will restore,
  The beautiful Cottage, and bonny Portmore.

Sallagh Island, the Deer Park, and ancient Lalloo,
Where good JEREMY TAYLOR oft-times wander'd through,
And Bellbrook so lovely, upon the lake shore;
Dear scenes of my youth, shall I e'er see you more?
  Gay Erin, my country, lives in my heart's core,
  Her ' green pastures, still waters,' and bonny Portmore.

When from scenes such as these fate decrees us to part,
Their memory, in sadness, close clings round the heart;
And the friends we leave there, too, can ne'er be forgot;
No! never in this life, whate'er be our lot.
  There's a halo around, ne'er seen elsewhere before,
  Of romance, o'er the lake scene and bonny Portmore.

NOTES.

'The Island Queen.'

An honorary title, graciously bestowed on Mrs. A. F. T⸻⸻,
by the residents of the neighbourhood, on the occasion of her welcome
visit to this interesting locality—the home of her fathers.

'The Round Tower.'

Ram's Island presents a fine specimen, forty feet high, of the ancient
Round Towers of Ireland; regarding which so much has of late been
written, and so little known. On opening the floor of this tower, some
years ago, a male human skeleton, imbedded in a white substance re-
sembling alabaster, was discovered, measuring in length seven feet,
It was forwarded to London.
Our poet MOORE, has, as in the instance of his loved 'Vale of Ovoca,
immortalised the old tower and lake scene, in the well-known
lines, viz :—

> 'On Lough Neagh's banks, as the fisherman strays,
>   When the clear cold eve's declining;
> He sees the round towers of other days,
>   In the wave beneath him shining.'

'The Ivy Tree,'

Which covers the base of the round tower with its broad green
leaves, has obtained a celebrity here, in the lines of the favourite old
song called ' Ballinderry,' viz :—

> 'It's pretty to be in bonny Ram's Island,
>   Sitting under the ivy tree.'

B

8

The concluding lines of the song, so anxiously expressive of the wanderer's wish to leave the Island, on the approach of night, is here added, viz :—

> 'The Lough is deep, I cannot wade it,
>   The night grows dark, I cannot stay;
> Oh! that I had a bonny barque,
>   To sail me over to Sandy Bay,'

The *air* of the forgoing song, '*Ballinderry*' is published in the third volume of the late lamented Mr. EDWARD BUNTING's 'Collection of Irish Music,' as is also, our favourite *air* of '*Bonny Portmore*,' appearing therein, under the title of '*Peggy na Levin.*' It may here be observed, that the same volume contains that soul-stirring composition by CAROLAN, called '*Doctor John Hart.*'

'Sandy Bay Harbour'

Is the usual place for Lake excursionists to obtain good boats. A branch of the Moravians—a sect justly esteemed by all, for their faithfulness, tolerance, and gentleness—have of late raised a respectable place of worship here; its tall picturesque gable overlooking the clear, pure, waters of the Lake. The grounds around it, are laid out in ornamental and shady walks. A school has been by them established here.

'Shane's Castle.'

Extensive ruins of the ancient seat of the O'NEILL family. Its finely wooded and beautiful park extends for miles along the shores of Lough Neagh. It is open to visiters, through the graciousness of its proprietor, Lord Viscount O'NEILL. The river Maine here, abounding with trout, empties itself into the lough. Angling is permitted. The Deer Park keeper's cottage, on the margin of the lake, near to Randalstown, has apartments nicely furnished for the free accommodation of visiters, by order of Lord O'NEILL.

'Sallagh Island,'

A small Island, situate near the interesting ruins of the late Rev. Bishop JEREMY TAYLOR's palace at Portmore. In a summer-house formerly on this Island, he wrote his celebrated work 'The Holy Living and Dying.' It may be interesting to know that his other residence in the neighbourhood, was 'Maralave Big House,' about a mile from Lisburn; a portion of which is yet habitable, particularly the bishop's parlour, curiously ornamented with the original fanciful heavy wainscotings just as he had last left it. The stone-covered clear spring well, at foot of the old terraced garden bank, behind the house, is in good preservation. There, in the spring time of the year, may be yet observed gay daffodils raising their yellow heads above the grass, as if to keep alive in our hearts, the memory of the dear good man, who had them planted there in the olden time.

'Talloo,'

The interesting ruins of an ancient place of worship, situate in the great Deer Park, at Portmore.

'The Lake.'

This beautiful sheet of water extends some twenty miles in length, and twelve in breadth; it is bounded by no less than five Counties, Antrim, Down, Armagh, Derry, and Tyrone; it covers about one hundred thousand acres; in some parts it is fifty feet deep. It is well stocked with wild ducks and other aquatic fowl, and contains large quantities of salmon trout and other fish. The strand abounds with beautiful pebbles, which take a high polish. The waters of this Lough are noted for their purity, as well as petrifying qualities. Specimens of petrified wood may be seen at Ram's Island.

There are various other interesting localities bordering on the Lake, as well as those here mentioned; amongst the rest is Langford Lodge and its charming grounds; Antrim Castle, and splendid park, with its old oak trees spreading their branches to the water's edge. It abounds in pheasants. Near to this, is another ancient round tower, eighty feet high, the roof is surmounted by a cone.

Moneyglass House, also in the vicinity, may be here mentioned, as being celebrated by the well-known and spirited *Planxty*, composed in this house by CAROLAN, in honour of an ancestor of the present proprietor; and also by DEAN SWIFT's well-known verses, written here, to the said *air*, and ending in these words, viz:—

> ' The good house, Moneyglass,
> Be sure you don't pass;
> Where there's mirth and good humour,
> And Bumper Squire Jones.'

A considerable degree of interest is attached to Brookhill House, in this locality, the seat of the late JAMES WATSON, Esq., J.P. and D.L, of the County Antrim. He was a gentleman of the good old school.

deservedly esteemed, highly respected, and his loss regretted by all.
He was well known here, by the honorary title of 'The Commodore,'
arising from his ancestor, the gallant Admiral WATSON, whose intre-
pidity in the East will long cause his memory to be venerated in the
United Kingdom.

In the north transept of Westminster Abbey, a magnificent monument is erected to the memory of ADMIRAL WATSON, where may be seen,
in the centre of a range of palm trees, an elegant figure of the Admiral
in a Roman toga, with a branch of palm in his right hand, receiving
the address of a prostrate figure, representing the Genius of Calcutta,
a place in the East Indies, memorable for the imprisonment of the
English Garrison in a black hole, where most of them perished, and
those that survived were released by the Admiral, and the town retaken
from the Nabob, in January, 1757. On the other side, is the figure, in
chains, of a native of Chandernagore, another place taken by th
Admiral, the March following.   On the front is this inscription:—

'To the Memory of Charles Watson,

VICE-ADMIRAL OF THE WHITE,

COMMANDER-IN-CHIEF OF HIS MAJESTY'S NAVY IN THE EAST INDIES,

Who died at Calcutta, August the 16th, 1757.

The East India Company, as a grateful testimony of the signal ad-
vantages which they obtained by his valour and prudent
conduct, caused this monument to be erected.'

Amongst so many pretty places, here may be noticed that of Glendona Lodge, situate a short distance from the lake; its extensive lawn
and favourite old oak tree in front, which 'the woodman has spared.'
The house is a good specimen of the neat comfortable dwellings erected
by the English and Scotch settlers in the old Lord CONWAY's time.
Whatever may be wanting in new fashioned architectural taste without, is amply compensated for, by the old-fashioned hospitality, the
kindness, and the fair faces within.

POSTSCRIPT.

————

On looking over the third volume of the late Mr. Edward Bunting's collection of Irish Music, referred to herein, I observed with some regret, that he had only been fortunate enough to obtain a few scattered lines of the original, ancient, curious, and very pleasing words attached to the sweet old *air* therein published, called '*My Bonny Cuckoo;*' and as I had learned the song correctly when very young, from a dear departed friend who, many a time and oft, sung it sweetly to me. My transcribing the words here, may prove acceptable to George Petrie, Esq., R.A., of Dublin, and others who take an interest in the like.

> ' My bonny cuckoo, I've found you true,
>   And through the woods I'll rove with you;
>   I'll rove with you until the next spring,
>   And then my cuckoo shall sweetly sing.
>   Cuckoo, cuckoo, let no one tell
>   Until that I settle my seasons well!
>
> ' But, cuckoo says, I must be gone,
>   For now cold winter is coming on,
>   With frost and snow, and stormy weather,
>   Which scatters the leaves and makes them wither;
>   It changes their hue to purple and yellow,
>   And makes them fly to find their fellow.

'The ash and the hazel will mourning, say,
My bonny cuckoo, don't go away;
Don't go away, but tarry here,
We'll make the summer last all the year;
   Cuckoo, cuckoo, let no one tell
   Untill that I settle my seasons well.

'When stormy winter is past and gone,
And April, with primroses, comes anon,
Cuckoo will return, and sweetly sing
In the woodland-chorus, that welcomes spring.
   Cuckoo, cuckoo, let no one tell
   Until that I settle my seasons well!'

It is a curious fact that the oldest English song now known was written in the time of Queen Elizabeth, on the same subject as the present one, 'An Address to the Cuckoo.'

Bonny Portmore.

Andante

forte

forte

pia

pia

D: C

Having in the foregoing pages alluded to the Old Irish Air
of "Bonny Portmore," I herewith beg leave to add an interesting
and expressive set of it, in the hope that it may be welcomed
by gentle readers who are blessed with a Musical taste, and
who take an interest in the Musick of

—————————— 'the land we love best,
'Tis the Land of our Fathers, our own darling West'

Gentle Reader,

HAVING in the foregoing pages, endeavoured, in some degree, to bring before your notice, the interesting scenery, and relics of other days, to be met with at Ram's Island and its vicinity, which, for many miles. around, may truly be called the Eden of Ireland; so great and so apparent is the general improvement, industry, and comfort everywhere observable, chiefly within this last five-and-twenty years. All this is well-known and admitted to be mainly attributable to the good taste, the energetic and kindly management, as well as the faithful tenant-right principles of the Very Rev. JAMES STANNUS, Dean of Ross, supported by the judicious and liberal concurrence of our esteemed landlord, the Marquis of HERTFORD.

Mrs. S. C. HALL, in her accredited work on Ireland, speaks in more flattering terms of the town of Lisburn, on the banks of the Lagan river, and the vicinity, than she does of any other part of the kingdom. The various approaches to this town, also the new wide streets, are ornamented by rows of spreading trees. Most of the villas, farm-houses, and neat cottages around, have jessamines, honeysuckles, and ever-blowing roses trained over their walls. The travellers' joy, *clematis*, and occasionally the broad-leafed Irish ivy, hanging in festoons over their entrance porch. And in the neatly-kept parterres in front, may be seen carnations, the gaudy hollyhock, and the rosemary 'that's for remembrance,' with other old favourites, not forgetting the occasional appearance of a modest little blue flower, spreading forth its delicate blossoms in a sunny corner, where may be sometimes seen in the twilight of a summer's evening, a gentle hand tending it, and a still gentler sweet voice, in a somewhat subdued tone, singing those well-known lines, viz.—

> 'Why, dearest, dost thou linger, far away from me,
> While pensive memory's finger ever points to thee?
> Over what mountains bounding—over what silent sea,
> With dangers dark, surrounding, oh! come back to me,
>   Oh! come back to me, my love, oh! come back to me,
>   Oh! come back, oh! come back, oh! come back to me.'

An occasional bee-hive may be also met with in the gardens; symbolical of the good order, awakened energy, self-reliance, and peaceful industry at home.

Before parting with you, gentle reader, allow me to assure you that any interest you may take in visiting Ram's Island and the country around, that interest will be heightened by the kind welcome of the inhabitants; of whom it may be truly said that 'heart speaks to heart.'

In bidding you adieu I shall conclude with the words of ROBBIE BURNS,

> " And each took of his several way,
>   In hopes to meet another day."

H. B.

NOTES

1   Laura's birthday was 18 October (letter from William Gladstone to Laura 18 October 1869) in *The Gladstone Diaries with cabinet minutes and prime-ministerial correspondence* edited by M.R.D. Foot and H.C.G. Matthew, 14 vols. (Oxford: Clarendon Press, 1968-94) [hereafter *Gladstone Diaries*], vol. 8, p. 562. On her marriage certificate, dated 21 January 1852, the word 'minor' is entered against her age i.e. she was then under 21 years of age. Her death certificate states that she died 30 May 1894 aged 62 years. The only birth date to fit all three statements is 18 October 1831.

2   From birth and death notices of Laura's brothers and sisters in the *Belfast Newsletter* identified by the addresses 'Bell Brook Glenavy' (1833, 1835, 1841) and 'Bell Brook near Glenavy' (1842).

3   Alfred Esmore, 'Laura Bell: the Life Romance of an Irish Adventuress' in Christmas 1913 issue of *The Lady of the House*, pp. 31-4 and 41 [hereafter Esmore, *Lady of the House*], p. 34.

4   Esmore, *Lady of the House*, p. 31 and *A Mid-Victorian Pepys: the letters and memoirs of Sir William Hardman* edited by S.M. Ellis (London: Cecil Palmer, 1923), p. 193, quoting an unnamed source.

5   Horace Wyndham, *Feminine Frailty* (London: Ernest Benn, 1929), p. 33.

6   Archibald Sparke in Notes and Queries 12S. XI. Sept. 16, 1922 p. 234 repeated by W.H. Holden *They Startled Grandfather* (London: British Technical and General Press, 1950) p. 121.

7   Letter 3 January 1870, *Gladstone Diaries*, vol. 8, p. 583.

8   Diary entry 7 June 1871, *Gladstone Diaries*, vol. 7, p. 505.

9   For further information on the Seymour-Conways, Marquesses of Hertford, and Sir Richard Wallace (who gave his name to the Wallace Collection, which his widow subsequently bequeathed to the British Nation), see Bernard Falk, *The Naughty Seymours: companions in folly and caprice* (London: Hutchinson, 1940), *Old Q's Daughter: a strange family history* (London: Hutchinson, 1951), and Donald Mallett *The Greatest Collector: Lord Hertford and the founding of the Wallace Collection* (London: Macmillan, 1979).

10 Sir Bernard Burke, *A Genealogical and Heraldic Dictionary of the Landed Gen-*

try of Great Britain and Ireland [hereafter Burke, *Landed Gentry*] (London: Henry Colburn, 1855) p. 1194. Although the title page ſtates 1855 it was aćtually published in parts between 1855 and 1858. The Thiſtlethwayte entry was repeated in the next edition (London: Harrison, 1863) p. 1495.

11   Esmore, *Lady of the House,* p. 34.

12   Cutting from the *Sphere* (unknown issue, 1927) in the Wallace Collećtion archive file on Laura Bell.

13   For further information on this fascinating charaćter see Henry Blyth *Old Q; The Rake of Piccadilly* (London: Weidenfeld & Nicolson, 1967) and Lewis Melville *The Star of Piccadilly: a memoir of William Douglas Fourth Duke of Queensberry* (London: Hutchinson, 1927). For a contemporary view of his exploits and miſtresses see the chapbook *Memoirs of the Life of His Grace the late Duke of Queensbery* [sic] *Humorously called Old Q* (London: T. Broom, *c.*1820).

14   Wyndham, *Feminine Frailty,* p. 33 and Henry J. Coke *Tracks of a Rolling Stone* (London: Smith Elder, 1905), p. 323.

15   Cutting from the *Wesleyan Times* n.d.

16   Esmore, *Lady of the House,* p. 31.

17   The rank of Captain seems to have originated in Burke, *Landed Gentry* (1855/8 edition). Esmore in *Lady of the House,* p. 34 ſtates that Laura's claim that her father was 'Captain Bell of the 4th Dragoon Guards' was a lie.

18   Private correspondence with M.R.D. Foot.

19   Esmore, *Lady of the House,* p. 31.

20   Burke, *Landed Gentry,* p. 1194.

21   Samuel Lewis, *A Topographical Dićtionary of Ireland ... with hiſtorical and ſtatiſtical descriptions,* 2 vols. and an atlas (London: S. Lewis, 1837), vol. 1, p. xi. Againſt the name of Robert Bell is an aſterisk indicating he ordered a large paper copy of the work (which was more expensive than the ordinary edition).

22   *Northern Whig,* date unknown but the letter is dated 1 December 1903 so it muſt have been published within a day or two of this date.

23   Esmore, *Lady of the House*, p. 34.

24   Conversation with Mr Nelson Bell

25   *Belfast Newsletter* 16 August 1842: 'On the 7th inst. in Dundalk, on his way to Dublin, Captain Robert Bell, of Bell Brook, near Glenavy, in the 70th year of his age, deeply regretted by all who had the pleasure of his acquaintance'.

26   Esmore, *Lady of the House*, p. 31.

27   *Ordnance Survey Memoirs of Ireland, vol. 21, Parishes of County Antrim VII, 1832-8 South Antrim*, edited by Angélique Day and Patrick McWilliams (Belfast: Institute of Irish Studies, 1993), p. 91.

28   Letter 5 Oct 1869, *Gladstone Diaries*, vol. 8, p. 560.

29   Gladstone Papers MS 2767 fo. 143-4.

30   Letter 1 October 1869, *Gladstone Diaries*, vol. 8, p. 558.

31   Letter 5 October 1869, *Gladstone Diaries*, vol. 8, p. 560.

32   Letter 7 October 1869, *Gladstone Diaries*, vol. 8, p. 561.

33   Letter 18 October 1869, *Gladstone Diaries*, vol. 8, p. 563.

34   Letter 1 October 1869, *Gladstone Diaries*, vol. 8, p. 559.

35   Esmore, *Lady of the House*, p. 32 mentions a woollen draper shop, conversation with J.F. Burns, who in his 'From Whoredom to Evangelism', *Lisburn Historical Society Journal*, vol. 2, 1979, p. 11 states that it was in the Mourning Department of the shop.

36   *Henderson's New Belfast Directory and Northern Repository for 1846-7* (Belfast: John Henderson, 1846), *Slater's National Commercial Directory of Ireland* (Manchester: Slater, 1846).

37   Wyndham, *Feminine Frailty*, p. 33.

38   The details of Laura's lovers in Belfast are all taken from Esmore, *Lady of the House*, p. 32, who is the solitary source for this information.

39   Esmore, *Lady of the House*, p. 32.

40   Esmore, *Lady of the House*, p. 32.

41   The Major and the Surgeon left Laura before she had arrived at her lodgings, which were owned by 'Mrs. D.' — letter 1 October 1869 *Gladstone Diaries*, vol. 8, p. 559. It is unclear whether Mrs D was just the owner of the lodgings, but given Laura's reputation she may have been an intermediary or procuress.

42   Esmore, *Lady of the House*, p. 32.

43   Letter 1 October 1869, *Gladstone Diaries*, vol. 8, p. 560.

44   In the *Northern Whig* 17 September 1846 the theatre manager Mr Cunningham announced that the scenic department had been placed under the superintendence of Mr Richard Thomas, and Mr Dearlove the artist. Again in the *Northern Whig* 16 October 1846 Mr Cunningham advertised that during the interval between the play and the farce the theatre would exhibit a view painted by Mr Dearlove from a sketch, taken on the spot, of the steamship *Great Britain*, which had run aground on the sands in Dundrum Bay on her maiden voyage. It had to be refloated and towed back to Bristol for repairs.

45   Esmore, *Lady of the House*, p. 32.

46   Coke, *Tracks of a Rolling Stone*, p. 323.

47   British Library Add. MS 44444, p. 200.

48   Esmore, *Lady of the House*, p. 32.

49   Henry Blyth, *Skittles: the last Victorian courtesan* (London: Rupert Hart-Davis, 1970), p. 43. Wilde (1815-76) spent an extended period increasing his medical expertise by studying in London, Vienna, Dresden and Heidelberg, returning to Dublin in 1841 to set up his practice in Westland Row. In the late 1840s when he met Laura Bell he would have been in his mid-thirties and unmarried.

50   Esmore, *Lady of the House*, p. 32.

51   Esmore, *Lady of the House*, p. 32.

52   Captain H.G. Hart, *The New Annual Army List for 1848* (London: John Murray, 1848), p. 237.

53   Blyth, *Skittles*, p. 43.

54   In the literature there are various spellings of his name — Jang Bahadur, Jung Bahadoor, Jung Bahadour etc. For further information on his life see John Whelpton, *Jang Bahadur in Europe* (Kathmandu: Shayogi, 1983), Laurence Oliphant, *A Journey to Katmandu* (London: John Murray, 1852) and H. Ambrose Oldfield, *Sketches from Nipal* (London: W.H. Allen, 1880).

55   Purushottam Sham Shere J.B. Rana, *Jung Bahadur Rana: the story of his rise to glory* (Delhi: Book Faith India, 1998), p. 59.

56   Rana, *Jung Bahadur Rana*, p. 63.

57   Esmore, *Lady of the House*, p. 32, where it is also referred to as Wilton Place. W. Carew Hazlitt also refers to Wilton Place in *Four Generations of a Literary Family*, 2 vols. (London: George Redway, 1897) vol. 2, p. 185. Holden in *They Startled Grandfather*, p. 122 suggests it was 4 Wilton Crescent, a house which belonged to Lord Bathurst (a relative of her future husband).

58   The earliest reference I have found to the specific amount is in Blyth, *Skittles*, p. 44.

59   Charles A. Dolph, *The Real 'Lady of the Camellias' and other women of quality* (London: Werner Laurie, 1927), p. 65.

60   Esmore, *Lady of the House*, p. 32.

61   Rana, *Jung Bahadur Rana*, p. 62.

62   Rana, *Jung Bahadur Rana*, p. 74.

63   Both versions are mentioned in Burns, *Lisburn Historical Society Journal*, pp. 16-17.

64   Duke of Portland, *Men, Women and Things, Memories of the Duke of Portland* (London: Faber and Faber, 1937), p. 260.

65   *Manitoba Daily Free Press*, 22 July 1885.

66   Blyth, *Skittles*, p. 44.

67   Wyndham, *Feminine Frailty*, p. 41.

130

68   *Manitoba Daily Free Press*, 22 July 1885.

69   The Salar Jung / Prince of Wales story appears in Dolph, *Lady of the Camellias*, p. 61-5 and is repeated by Wyndham, *Feminine Frailty*, p. 37, who claimed it was originally published some time previously in a ladies' fashion journal.

70   Rana, *Jung Bahadur Rana*, pp. 144-6.

71   Wyndham, *Feminine Frailty*, p. 37, Dolph, *Lady of the Camellias*, pp. 58-65 and Coke, *Tracks of a Rolling Stone*, p. 323.

72   Wyndham, *Feminine Frailty*, p. 37.

73   'A Woman of no Importance', *Recollections and Reflections* (London: Eveleigh Nash and Grayson, 1921), p. 27.

74   Coke, *Tracks of a Rolling Stone*, p. 323.

75   Sir Francis Burnand, *Records and Reminiscences Personal and General*, 2 vols. (London: Methuen, 1904), vol. 1, pp. 237-8. A 'tiger' was a page boy with a striped waistcoat.

76   Cyril Pearl, *The Girl with the Swansdown Seat* (London: Frederick Muller, 1955), p. 143.

77   Esmore, *Lady of the House*, p. 32.

78   Hazlitt, *Four Generations*, vol. 2, p. 185.

79   Wyndham, *Feminine Frailty*, p. 35.

80   Wyndham, *Feminine Frailty*, p. 35.

81   Burnand, *Records and Reminiscences*, vol. 1, p. 238. Sharpe died in Dover Workhouse in 1856.

82   For further information on Laura's rivals see Polly Binder, *The Truth about Cora Pearl* (London: Weidenfeld & Nicolson, 1986), Susan Griffin, *The Book of Courtesans* (London: Pan Books, 2001), Katie Hickman, *Courtesans* (London: Harper Perennial, 2003), Virginia Rounding, *Grandes Horizontales: the lives and legends of four nineteenth-century courtesans* (London: Bloomsbury, 2003).

83   *Platteville Independant American*, 10 October 1851.

84 *Burlington Weekly Hawk-eye*, 11 February 1865. John Cumming (1807-81) was the minister of Crown Court Church, Covent Garden. He was famed for his preaching and his best known published work was *The Great Tribulation* (1859). Both William Thackery and George Elliot condemned him as a bigot.

85 Mrs [Tryphena] Thistlethwayte, *Memoirs and Correspondence of Dr. Henry Bathurst* (London: Richard Bentley, 1853), p. 310.

86 Thistlethwayte, *Memoirs*, pp. 159-68. The pamphlet, dated 12 February 1804, was titled *The Justice and policy of Granting a full and complete toleration to the Roman Catholics of Ireland asserted by a Clergyman of the Church of England, in a letter to the Right Hon. Lord Grenville*.

87 Thistlethwayte, *Memoirs*, pp. 75-91.

88 Lord Bathurst and Laura's niece Emily Thistlethwayte.

89 Esmore, *The Lady of the House*, p. 33.

90 Esmore, *The Lady of the House*, p. 33 which erroneously states that Thomas Thistlethwayte died in 1852.

91 Quoted in Jean Gilliland, *Gladstone's 'Dear Spirit' Laura Thistlethwayte* (Oxford: privately published, 1994), p. 8.

92 Gilliland, *Gladstone's 'Dear Spirit'*, p. 8.

93 Henry Vizetelly, *Glances Back through Seventy Years*, 2 vols. (London: Kegan Paul Trench Trübner & Co., 1893), vol. 2, p. 28.

94 The photograph of the Oval Drawing Room is reproduced in Graham Reynolds, *Wallace Collection Catalogue of Miniatures*, (London: Trustees of the Wallace Collection, 1980), pp. 24-5, where the Girard miniature is numbered 51.

95 Correspondence by Brian Stewart in the Wallace Collection archive file on Laura Bell.

96 Roslyn Robinson, 'From Courtesan to Christendom' in *New Ulster*, No. 24 November 1994, p. 8.

97   Mrs Godfrey Pearse [Cecilia Maria Pearse], *The Enchanted Past* (London: Chapman & Hall, 1926), pp. 151-2.

98   Correspondence by Brian Stewart in the Wallace Collection archive file on Laura Bell.

99   *More Uncensored Recollections by the author of 'Uncensored Recollections' and 'Things I Shouldn't tell'* [anon but actually Julian Osgood Field] (London: Eveleigh Nash & Grayson, 1926), p. 259.

100   Correspondence by the Lord Ironside in the Wallace Collection archive file on Laura Bell.

101   Reynolds, *Wallace Collection Miniatures,* p. 269, footnote 2.

102   Correspondence by Mrs Sarah Thistlethwayte in the Wallace Collection archive file on Laura Bell.

103   Esmore, *Lady of the House,* p. 33.

104   *Ordnance Survey Memoirs of Ireland, vol. 21, Co. Antrim VII,* p. 83.

105   James Clarke, *Historical Record and Regimental Memoir of the Royal Scots Fusiliers* (Edinburgh: Banks & Co., 1885), pp. 48-51.

106   Esmore, *Lady of the House,* pp. 33-4.

107   He may be the Henry Bell from Crumlin who appears above Laura's father in the subscribers list to Lewis's *Topographical Dictionary* in 1837, or who answered a query concerning the residence of Jeremy Taylor, Bishop of Down and Connor, in the *Ulster Journal of Archaeology,* Series 1, vol. 2, p. 285 (1854) and vol. 3, p. 81 (1855).

108   Charles Watson, *The Story of the United Parishes of Glenavy, Camlin and Tullyrusk* (Belfast: McCaw, Stevenson & Orr Linenhall Works, 1892), p. 59. The work by Mr and Mrs S.C. Hall was *Ireland, its character, scenery etc.*

109   *Belfast Newsletter,* 18 October 1854.

110   Esmore, *Lady of the House,* p. 34.

111   Frederick Thistlethwayte's marriage certificate.

112 The house number was 100 — private address book of the 4th Marquess of Hertford, the Wallace Collection.

113 *Burlington Weekly Hawk-eye*, 11 February 1865, which repeats the story it obtained from a correspondent for the *New York Herald*.

114 Wyndham, *Feminine Frailty*, p. 47.

115 Lady St Helier [Mary Jeune], *Memories of Fifty Years* (London: Edward Arnold, 1909), p. 43.

116 Quoted in Wyndham, *Feminine Frailty*, p. 50.

117 St Helier, *Memories*, p. 44.

118 St Helier, *Memories*, p. 45.

119 Reproduced in Ellis, *Mid-Victorian Pepys*, p. 192.

120 Reproduced in Wyndham, *Feminine Frailty*, p. 54.

121 The newspaper cutting (of unknown date) is pasted into Gladstone Papers MS 2759 fo. 38, and the words 'Wesleyan Times ' are written above it.

122 Newspaper cutting pasted into Gladstone Papers MS 2759 fo. 38.

123 Wyndham, *Feminine Frailty*, pp. 48, 50 and 57.

124 Dolph, *Lady of the Camellias*, p. 58.

125 Wyndham, *Feminine Frailty*, p. 51.

126 *Fifty Years of Fleet Street being the Life and Recollections of Sir John R. Robinson*, compiled and edited by Frederick Moy Thomas (London: McMillan & Co., 1904), p. 279.

127 Quoted in Wyndham, *Feminine Frailty*, p. 49.

128 Quoted in Wyndham, *Feminine Frailty*, p. 57.

129 Quoted in Dolph, *Lady of the Camellias*, p. 53.

130 Esmore, *Lady of the House*, p. 34.

131 Lord Congleton's pedantic form of Christian belief is exemplified by the following tale: One day Lord Congleton had posted in the area of Dublin where he owned many houses a message that if his tenants came to his office on a certain day before 12 noon, he would forgive their debts. None of the poor tenants, many of whom were out of work and owed large amounts of back-rent, turned up on the day. Just before noon one man ventured to approach Lord Congleton and informed him that he expected to be forgiven his debt. Lord Congleton wrote 'Paid in full' on the rent paper. The man returned to the crowd and told them of his good fortune, but it was now just after noon and Lord Congleton had locked the door so none could get their debts cancelled. The moral of the story was that just as the poor people missed out on having their debts cancelled because they did not trust Lord Congleton's word, they could miss out on having their sins forgiven by God because they did not believe in the Lord Jesus. Astoundingly, this tale and its moral are still being circulated by evangelical Christians on the Internet.

132 Esmore, *Lady of the House,* p. 34.

133 *National Union Catalog of Pre-1956 Imprints,* vol. 590, p. 256.

134 www.recmusic.org/lieder/b/byron/fairwell.hml, accessed 5 December 2001.

135 *Survey of London,* ed. F.H.W. Sheppard, vol. XL *The Grosvenor Estate in May-fair, Part II: The Buildings* (London: The Athlone Press, 1980), pp. 112-5, 130-3.

136 Private correspondence with M.R.D. Foot who informed me that he was given the information by the Gladstone family archivist, the late A.T. Bassett, who believed the story to be true.

137 Letter 6 January 1874, *Gladstone Diaries,* vol. 12, p. 465.

138 Letters 22 March 1875, 6 April 1875, *Gladstone Diaries,* vol. 12, p. 471.

139 Hazlitt, *Four Generations,* vol. 2, p. 185.

140 *More Uncensored Recollections,* pp. 259-60. On p. 261 the author described the moneylender Sam Lewis as 'the astute and genial cash conjurer of Cork Street'.

141 Holden, *They Startled Grandfather,* pp. 125-6.

142 Coke, *Tracks of a Rolling Stone*, p. 323.

143 The official biography by John Martineau, *The Life of Henry Pelham Fifth Duke of Newcastle 1811-1864* (London: John Murray, 1908), omits all details surrounding the divorce. For further details see Virginia Surtees, *A Beckford Inheritance: the Lady Lincoln scandal* (Salisbury: Michael Russell, 1977) and F.D. Munsell, *The Unfortunate Duke Henry Pelham, Fifth Duke of Newcastle, 1811-1864* (Columbia: University of Missouri Press, 1985).

144 Diary entry 5 February 1865, *Gladstone Diaries*, vol. 6, p. 332.

145 Esmore, *Lady of the House*, p. 41.

146 Letter 8 November 1885, *Gladstone Diaries*, vol. 12, p. 514.

147 Letter 29 November 1889, *Gladstone Diaries*, vol. 12, p. 524.

148 Esmore, *Lady of the House*, p. 41.

149 Will of Laura Thistlethwayte, dated 29 June 1892.

150 Conversation with Mr George Farnham.

151 Wyndham, *Feminine Frailty*, p. 46, where he states the incident occurred in 1856.

152 Coke, *Tracks of a Rolling Stone*, pp. 323-4.

153 Diary entry 1 May 1887, *Gladstone Diaries*, vol. 12, p. 33.

154 Letter 16 March 1871, *Gladstone Diaries*, vol. 12, p. 441. The Petrarchs were books Laura had lent Gladstone. The general tone of letter and appended comment are typical of the surviving correspondence.

155 Letter 20 August 1871, *Gladstone Diaries*, vol. 12, p. 445.

156 Letter 6 September 1871, *Gladstone Diaries*, vol. 12, p. 446.

157 Letter 17 November 1871, *Gladstone Diaries*, vol. 12, p. 450.

158 Letter 14 August 1874, *Gladstone Diariess* vol. 12 p. 468.

159 Diary entry 2 July 1869, *Gladstone Diaries*, vol. 7, p. 90.

160 Letter 25 October 1869, *Gladstone Diaries*, vol. 8, p. 569 mentions fascicles XXI-XXIII, which concern Laura's London life.

161 Letter 18 October 1869, *Gladstone Diaries*, vol. 8, p. 563.

162 Letter 26 February 1893, *Gladstone Diaries*, vol. 12, p. 530.

163 Esmore, *Lady of the House*, p. 41.

164 Letter 27 October 1869, *Gladstone Diaries*, vol. 8 p. 572.

165 Letter 1 November 1869, *Gladstone Diaries*, vol. 8, p. 576.

166 Letter 13 November 1869, *Gladstone Diaries*, vol. 8, p. 578.

167 Diary entries 2-4 October 1875, *Gladstone Diaries*, vol. 9, p. 71.

168 Diary entry 26 February 1878, *Gladstone Diaries*, vol. 9, p. 294.

169 http://129.62.34.181/layard/xml.php?fn=18870323.xml, accessed 30 June 2005. The date of the party was 9 March 1887. Gladstone recorded in his diary that he held a conversation with Sir Harry Ponsonby, brother of Barbara and Georgina Ponsonby (who was confidante of Mrs Thistlethwayte). Diary entry 9 March 1878, *Gladstone Diaries*, vol. 12, p. 17.

170 Lady St Helier, *Memories*, p. 256.

171 'A Woman of no Importance', *Recollections*, pp. 37-8.

172 Coke, *Tracks of a Rolling Stone*, p. 323.

172 Wyndham, *Feminine Frailty*, p. 44.

174 Letter 30 August 1878, *Gladstone Diaries*, vol. 12, p. 486.

175 Wyndham, *Feminine Frailty*, p. 44.

176 Wyndham, *Feminine Frailty*, pp. 45-6.

177 Wyndham, *Feminine Frailty*, p. 47.

178 Gladstone Papers MS2768 fo. 99-101, undated letter Laura to Gladstone.

179 *More Uncensored Recollections,* p. 261.

180 Gladstone Papers MS2768 fo. 88.

181 Gladstone Papers MS2768 fo. 89 — letter 4 April 1879 Frederick Thistlethwayte to Gladstone.

182 Gladstone Papers MS2768 fo. 99-101 undated letter Laura to Gladstone.

183 Letter 10 April 1879, *Gladstone Diaries,* vol. 12, pp. 487-8.

184 Letter 25 April 1879, *Gladstone Diaries,* vol. 12, p. 489.

185 Letter 3 May 1879, *Gladstone Diaries,* vol. 12 p. 490.

186 Gladstone Papers MS2768 fo. 103 undated letter Laura to Gladstone.

187 The *Morning Post* 9 August 1887, quoted in Dolph, *Lady of the Camellias,* p. 55.

188 *Gladstone Diaries,* vol. 12, p. 59, footnote 4.

189 Gilliland, *Gladstone's 'Dear Spirit',* p. 26.

190 Diary of Robert John Bell, this quotation kindly provided by his descendant Stephen C. Bell.

191 Gladstone Papers MS2770 fo. 104, newspaper obituary (undated).

192 Diary entry 18 January 1887, *Gladstone Diaries,* vol. 12, p.33.

193 Woodbine Cottage was first mentioned by Gladstone 20 July 1886, last specific mention 17 May 1894, a fortnight before her death.

194 7 December 1896, *Gladstone Diaries,* vol. 13, p. 428.

195 For further details of the case see the chapter 'Libel on a Dead Prime Minister' in H. Montgomery Hyde, *Their Good Names: twelve cases of libel and slander* (London: Hamish Hamilton, 1970).

196 Wyndham, *Feminine Frailty,* p. 60.

197 *The World. A Journal for Men and Women*, No. 1,040 Wednesday June 6, 1894.

198 Holden, *They Startled Grandfather*, p. 134.

199 In her Will the following bequests were made: a picture of Lord Bathurst Bishop of Norwich to Lord Bathurst; to the head of the Normanton family a picture of Lord Normanton; to her niece Emily Thistlethwayte a picture of Mrs Grace; personal effects (including books) to Lord Edward Pelham Clinton, with a request that he provides Woodbine Cottage as a retreat for clergymen of all denominations (there is no evidence of this having happened).
Annuities: £100 Miss Rebecca Mary Hamilton (Springfield Villa, 9 Greville Rd. Kilburn); £200 to her niece Louisa Vernon 36 Elgin Avenue Paddington); £100 to her maid; £50 to her head-servant.
Legacies: £500 Rebecca Mary Hamilton; £500 Harriet Furney; £1,500 George Tournay Biddulph; £2,500 Charles Innes; £3,000 Miss Milita Ponsonby; £3,000 to 'my relative' General Frederick Seymour; £4,000 representative of the late Sir Fitzroy Kelly; £5,000 General Ponsonby (Milita Ponsonby's brother).

200 Dolph, *Lady of the Camellias*, p. 70.

201 Isaac W. Ward writing (as Belfastiensis) a letter dated 1 December 1903 in the *Northern Whig* (date unknown). The story was repeated by Esmore, *Lady of the House*, p. 41.

202 Private correspondence with Nelson Bell and Stephen C. Bell.

203 PRONI mic 1/44 Glenavy Parish Register.

204 Esmore, *Lady of the House*, p. 31.

205 Wyndham, *Feminine Frailty*, p. 59.

INDEX

Thus endeth the ſtory of *Laura Bell,*
brought to completion by Anthony Drennan
on the firſt day of November 2007 and published abroad
by means of the printing art that it may be known to many.
Studious reader, if your knowledge of this ſtory is greater than mine
or if by chance you should ſtumble upon any alteration, transposition,
inversion or omission of letters, grammatical inexaƈtitude, or incorreƈtness
in this work, do not reproach me therefor if you do not praise
me for the great trouble which I have expended.
Perfeƈtion reigns only in God.